GOING FO
BLACK BELT

GOING FOR BLACK BELT

TONY GUMMERSON

STANLEY PAUL

London Sydney Auckland Johannesburg

Stanley Paul & Co. Ltd

An imprint of Century Hutchinson Ltd
20 Vauxhall Bridge Road, London SW1V 2SA

Century Hutchinson Australia (Pty) Ltd
20 Alfred Street, Milsons Point, Sydney 2061

Century Hutchinson New Zealand Limited
PO Box 40–086, Glenfield, Auckland 10

Century Hutchinson South Africa (Pty) Ltd
PO Box 337, Bergvlei 2012, South Africa

First published 1990

Set in Times & Helvetica by Tek Art Ltd, Croydon
Printed and bound in Great Britain by
Scotprint Ltd, Musselburgh

British Library Cataloguing in Publication Data
Gummerson, Tony
Going for the black belt: the key to success in
the martial arts and combat sports
1. Martial arts
I. Title
796.8

ISBN 0 09 174007 X

Contents

	PAGE
Acknowledgements	6
Training Theory and the Martial Arts	7
Introduction to the Martial Arts	9
Strength Training	13
Weight Training for the Martial Arts	16
Progressive Resistance Training	18
Notes on the Programmes	19
Advanced Weight Training	26
Strength Training Without Equipment	27
Strength Training – Variations on a Theme	37
Plyometrics	37
Speed	60
Speed Training	62
Speed Training – Some Further Considerations	64
Flexibility	66
Flexibility Training	70
Endurance	89
Applying Endurance to Training	90
Endurance Training	91
(P)Sychology	95
Skill	96
The Martial Arts from a Fitness Point of View	99
Food for Thought	106
Rehabilitation after Injury	116
Writing the Programme	120
Fitness Tests and Measurements	128

Acknowledgements

It would have been impossible to produce this book without the considerable help of a great many people who have been generous with their time, knowledge and expertise. However, there have been particular individuals and organisations which merit a special word of thanks:

David Mitchell was responsible for drawing me back into the world of martial arts and has been a source of constant inspiration and a 'fount of wisdom'. He has been an invaluable source of specific martial art knowledge and practice.

The Martial Arts Commission, for their help in providing me with the opportunity to further my understanding of the martial arts.

Carl Johnson, British Amateur Athletics Board ('BAAB') National Coach, who has given much support to my interest in coach education.

Wilf Paish, former BAAB National Coach, who nurtured my performance in sport and kindled a desire for a deeper understanding of the training process.

All the martial arts governing bodies who have allowed me the opportunity to learn from them, and without whose kindness and goodwill this book would never have been written. Particularly to Professor Robert Clark and the BJJA.

I would like to thank Pippa Mole and Brian McAninly for helping with the photographs for the various sections, and especially Alan Campbell and Carl Norman, both of the BJJA, for the cover.

Training Theory and the Martial Arts

The difficulty with any theory is putting it into practice! Even if, as with martial arts, there is a willingness to take on board new ideas, methods and practices, the actual application of such knowledge is often hindered by sports science jargon and academic overtones. With the best will in the world, the committed coach/student does not have the time or opportunity to engage in research into training methods, for the simple reason that all their available time is spent in actual practice. Martial artists are practically orientated by their very nature, for one of the reasons why they took up their discipline in the first place was to get away from sedentary and mentally-orientated activity. However, many coaches and students now recognise that they can make their time in training more productive by the application of new ideas.

This book is aimed at bridging the gap which exists between theory and practice. Each section will discuss one of the components of fitness and it will be split into three parts:

- A brief discussion of the main aspects involved with that particular fitness component. This will be general in nature and hopefully not too academic.
- The specific application of that element to martial art will be identified.
- A series of activities and exercises will be described which will allow the student and coach to see their application in the training situation. Suggestions on how to further modify and develop these activities and exercises will also be made.

The section entitled 'Writing the Programme' will discuss all of these elements with respect to creating a training schedule specific to the needs and demands of the individual student.

Before attempting to discuss the specific aspects of fitness and conditioning, it is probably as well to look at the general nature of the martial arts and their requirements. The first problem that any martial art student encounters is the fact that each art is different in both the techniques involved, and in the physical demands made upon the individual. For example, martial arts such as karate emphasise kicks, punches and blocks which involve little opponent contact; others, such as judo, use wrestling and locking techniques and are thus predominantly involved in opponent contact. In activities such as kendo, the essential element is the specific use of a weapon. Therefore it is a nonsense to speak of the training requirements for martial arts, since each has its own particular needs. Because of the highly specialised nature of some activities practised, there will be even more variation! The individual contribution of each of the aspects of fitness to the individual martial arts will be discussed in the appropriate sections.

Introduction to the Martial Arts

The history of the oriental martial arts goes back many centuries and the fascination which these arts evoke in their followers is not just based on the various fighting techniques and skills involved, but also on the mystery, legends, myths and historical development of their particular school. Most martial art students are equally interested in the culture and history of the country of origin and the evolution of their particular style into that which is practised today. Of all the many sports which are enthusiastically participated in, this all-embracing interest is unique.

The martial arts are set aside from other sports and activities by a second unique feature arising out of their historical tradition. That is, the passing on of skills from one individual to another has always been based on the simple premise that the teacher is a highly skilled exponent in his own right. The ability to teach others is primarily based upon the teacher's own practical experiences. Whereas this is a strength, insofar as much experience and expertise is passed down from one to another, it does not always follow that it has been done in the most efficient and effective fashion.

It has now become generally acknowledged that just because a martial artist has a high degree of technical and practical ability, it does not necessarily follow that he has the ability to communicate those skills and knowledge to others. In fact, the most skilful practitioners are generally those gifted with a high degree of natural ability. However, the fact that they have this natural aptitude does not guarantee them a clear understanding of those martial artists who experience problems with practice, or who are not so gifted, committed, enthusiastic, or dedicated. Similarly, years of involvement in martial art practice may not be taken as indicative of ability or experience in teaching others.

The tradition of passing skills from master to student has resulted in secrecy based upon mystical, personal, physical, psychological and financial factors. This secrecy means that there has been little in the way of interchange of ideas and knowledge. In fact, it has led to much introspection, and little heed has been paid to the potential contribution that other sporting disciplines might have to offer in the development of martial art skills and techniques.

Martial art tradition is based on what one might term 'Military Darwinism'. This simply means that effective practices have been incorporated, whilst those which were less than effective have eliminated themselves!

Until now, it can be said that the evolution of martial art has been quite effective despite its apparent lack of organised development. However, the last twenty years have seen a revolution, not just in the numbers of participants in sport in general and the martial arts in particular, but also in the analysis of those sporting activities in an attempt to improve the standard of performance at all levels. Sport has provided an opportunity for scientists to apply scientific principles to both the preparation for, and performance in, the competitive situation. Sports science has developed along various lines, and in particular, in biomechanics, psychology, nutrition, physiology and sports medicine. The desire for ever-increasing standards of performance has meant that both athlete and coach now turn ever more frequently to the sports scientists for help.

Though the present high standard of performance in martial art is mainly due to the application of traditional methods to both instruction and preparation, it is my belief that a much more effective approach could be undertaken if the relevant areas of sports science were investigated and, where appropriate, adopted.

Whereas it is perfectly correct to say that the currently high status of martial arts is firmly rooted in the past, I have no doubt that its future achievements will be based on a willingness to make use of increased knowledge in the area of sports science. The contribution to be made by such knowledge will not only assure the continued evolution of martial art at the highest technical level, but it will also benefit every student, whatever his level of proficiency and commitment.

Interestingly, many 'modern concepts' of coaching theory are already found in ancient martial art practice. In fact, most coaches use many of the techniques of effective and efficient instruction without being consciously aware of it! However, not all coaches practise or are aware of all those elements of good coaching which are so important in the development of the individual student's standard of performance.

Several factors have to be taken into account when assessing the quality of the overall performance.

The most important element in the qualitative assessment of performance is the student himself! His level of commitment, state of health, level of ability and potential have to be considered at all stages of development. The coach must possess the knowledge to teach that student at and to the level which he demands. The two must work together as a team to produce the optimum conditions for improvement. They must also have the assistance, where appropriate, of medical and sports scientists in order to ensure continued systematic development. Having said that, the best efforts of all concerned will be of little value without an adequate venue for training, competition and ancillary activities.

Ultimately, the standard of performance attained by a student is directly related to the time invested in preparation. Not only is the total amount of time critical, but the coach also needs to know which part of the day is available for training, and which period the student is in with respect to both long- and short-term planning. The effect of the menstrual cycle on female performers also needs to be considered.

Diagram 1 Human Daily Rhythms

Body function	Time of peak activity
brain	11 a.m. – 1 p.m.
hormones	11 a.m. – 1 p.m.
temperature	3 p.m.
weight	6 p.m.
heart rate	4 p.m.
respiration	2.30 p.m.
physical activity	3.30 p.m.

These times indicate the normal peak value of a particular body function. The times of lowest function can be assumed to occur 12 hours later.

Though it might be argued that a scientific approach to preparation is the best path to improved performance, the role of the coach must never be undervalued. Coaches must make themselves familiar with current training theory and they must also possess the sensitivity to be able to apply that theory to each and every individual, so as to help them to achieve their full potential. Diagram 2 shows some of the attributes that coaching requires. The application of the correct mix of these will create the best possible relationship between coach and student and will lead to optimum performance.

The following chapters will attempt to identify those essential elements which contribute to safe, effective, efficient and successful coaching. These elements are known as the 'S' factors, in an attempt to simplify what is a potentially difficult topic to come to terms with.

Diagram 2 The 'S' Factors

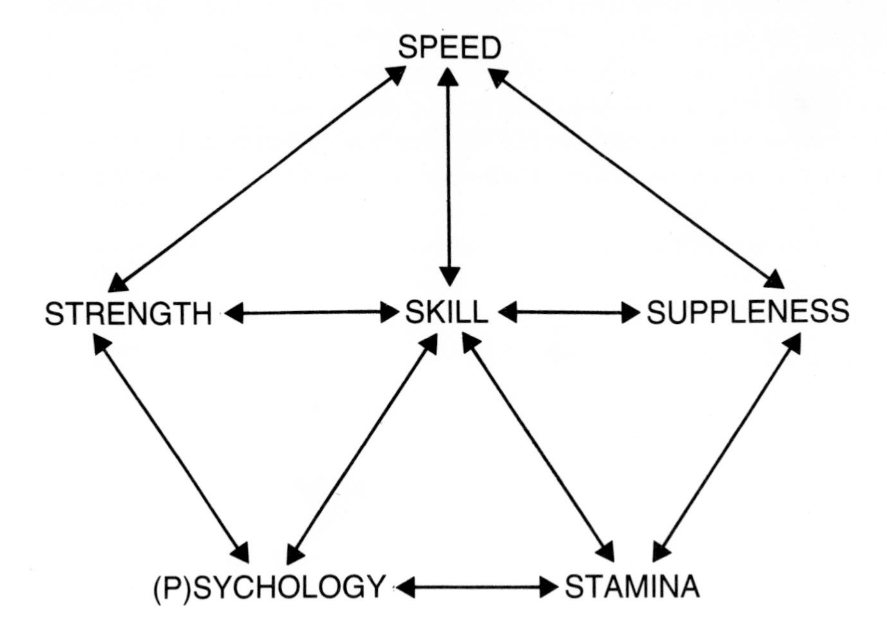

Though each and every coach might have his own understanding of what these 'S' factors are, they are normally given as:

Strength	**Speed**	**Stamina**
Suppleness	**Skill**	**(P)Sychology**

It is not enough to understand each element in isolation. Rather, one needs to know how they can all be integrated to produce the ideal mix for each martial art and each student. Each section of the book will offer ideas for training and competition preparation, and armed with that knowledge, the capable coach will be able to construct more enlightened schedules.

It is not possible to look in depth at physiology, psychology, mechanics and sports medicine. My aim is to show the coach practical applications of such fields. Each section will introduce the main principles involved, and I will then identify a series of exercises and activities which will bring about the desired effect. It is for the coach/student to assess areas of particular interest to them, and to identify the specific type of activity which best suits their needs. Lack of space prevents all exercises being listed, but hopefully the imaginative coach will be able to see how ideas might be developed to suit his own needs and situation.

Strength Training

The first problem facing the martial artist/coach who is interested in developing strength is to consider very carefully just which type of strength they mean. You see, the term 'strength' can be applied to such different things as:

- the instantaneous generation of force in breaking techniques.
- the ability to endure fatigue in competition, gradings and training where strength has to be constantly generated in order to perform the skill or technique.

It might be helpful to look at a few definitions of strength in order to clarify the position:

Strength 'The force that a muscle or group of muscles can exert against a resistance.'

Maximum Strength 'The greatest force that the neuromuscular system is capable of exerting in a single, maximal voluntary contraction.'

Relative Strength 'Maximum strength as a function of body weight.'

Elastic Strength 'The ability of the muscles to act explosively.'

Strength Endurance 'The ability to express strength in an ever-increasing climate of fatigue.'

Local Muscular Endurance 'The ability to maintain a work-rate in an ever-increasing state of fatigue at a local level.'

Willpower 'The ability of the student to concentrate on the maximum voluntary effort needed to achieve maximum/optimum strength.'

As you can see, there are several types of strength, each one highly specific, and the martial artist/coach much be very much aware of the type/s of strength required. The situation becomes even more complicated when one looks at the various different ways of gaining those specific strengths. Usually, only two types of training are identified – weight or circuit training – but this is far from comprehensive. Strength training relies on the principle that the load which an individual works against becomes greater as strength levels increase. An appropriate term for this would be 'Progressive Resistance Training' and examples include the use of:

weighted jackets	ankle and wrist weights
sand-filled bags	medicine balls
elastic ropes	pulleys
ropes	heavy boots
pulling tyres	log work
stones/rocks	sand dune running
surf running	hill running
step running	Bullworkers
Nautilus machines	springs
Dial-Ex machines	multi-gyms
pneumatic machines	barbells
dumbbells	gymnasium equipment

The committed coach can use a whole array of equipment and facilities to achieve the specific types of strength required. Only a lack of imagination and application limit their use.

There are, however, certain principles that must be considered when designing a strength training programme designed to produce a specific result.

The first principle to bear in mind is that of 'overload'. In order to continue improving strength levels, the load must be increased, such that muscles are working to their limit and are, in fact, being overloaded. This systematic and progressive increase in loading brings about optimum levels of strength acquisition.

The second principle is that intensive strength training must not follow a period of fatiguing activity. This is because the muscles lose their elasticity as waste products build up and any activity which then calls for fast powerful movements becomes potentially dangerous.

The third principle is the amount of recovery required, not just between bouts of activity, but between strength training days. Whereas muscles need to be overloaded on the day, sufficient time must then be allowed for recovery between training units. In fact, a rest period of at least 24 hours must be allowed for in most cases. The best scheme is to train for strength every other day, with the period of training in between set aside for something like technique work.

No one type of training is better than any other. Each contributes in its own right to a specific type of strength, or situation. It is for the good coach to choose the type of training required to bring about the desired result.

Not only are there specific types of strength, but it is important that the coach realises how the muscles actually work to produce force. Broadly speaking, muscles work, or contract, in two ways:

Isotonically The muscle shortens its length because it can generate more force than the resistance it is working against. This is typically shown when joints bend or straighten through their full range.

Isometrically The muscle does not change in length because the force it generates is equal to the load. Muscles used in posture and supportive or resistive activity exemplify this action.

However, it has recently been recognised that muscles can work in a third way:

Isokinetically The muscle works at its maximum throughout the entire range of movement – either shortening, or lengthening.

The principle of isokinetic muscle action has been linked by some coaches and physiologists to what is called 'Plyometrics'. This depends on the lengthening of the muscle against a load (usually body weight), followed by a rapid contraction. The muscle undergoes a form of contraction when it is prestretched in this way, and this allows a much quicker and generally more powerful response.

We are now at a point where we can summarise the decisions that the coach/student must make in order to achieve the required strength. These are:

- what type of strength is required?
- what type of muscle action is needed to produce that type of strength?
- which exercises will be best suited to the development of that type of strength?
- how many repetitions of the exercise are required?
  how many groups of repetitions?
  how much recovery?
- how much time is available?
- what facilities are available?

Weight Training for the Martial Arts

Most coaches today realise that strength training in some form or other has a vital role to play in any student's training programme. Strength training, or more accurately 'Progressive Resistance Training', manifests itself in many forms, any one of which may be relevant to an individual's specific needs. Weight training, as such, is only one of those forms.

Whereas most coaches would suggest any of several strengthening activities, there are few who would specify weight training and even fewer who would identify specific routines! It is to the credit of coaches, perhaps, that they shy away from weight training for their students because they feel that it involves an element of danger, especially for the young. They may also believe that specialist knowledge is required.

While it is true that increasing the load or resistance against which an individual has to work does involve an element of risk, the same is true of all training activities! Providing certain basic guidelines on safety are observed, there is no reason why a weight training programme cannot be undertaken. I have attempted to draw the essential safety guidelines together in a simplified form. Note that many of these are common not only to other forms of strength training, but to all physical activities in which the student may participate.

The Ten Commandments

1. Always ensure that the floor area is clear of loose weights, collars and any other items which might cause obstruction. Make certain that collars are tight on the bar and where appropriate, that 'spotters' (training partners), are ready to take the bar should the need arise. Good safe technique must not be sacrificed for heavier loads. Always ensure that a comprehensive warm-up precedes a training session. This must pay particular attention to mobility.

2. With young students, the emphasis should be on general strength. There is no reason for placing heavy loads on the shoulders until the student is at least 18 years of age (modern equipment can ensure that this never happens!). Attention should be paid to those muscles which control and support the spine.

3. If weights are taken on the shoulders, then the back must be kept straight. The spine must not curve and neither should there be rounding of the shoulders. If this guideline is ignored, then serious injury may be caused.
4. The training load for women should be increased at a slower rate than for men.
5. There is a serious risk of injury, especially with heavy loadings, if there has been an inadequate warm-up or load progression.
6. Strength training with heavy loads causes the muscles to become fatigued, and they will temporarily lose their elasticity. The general rule is, DON'T follow severe strength training with speed or mobility work.
7. Knee injuries can occur from poor squatting, particularly with heavy loads at full flexion. Vary squats with hamstring curls, quad raises, steps-ups and perhaps more dynamic exercises.
8. Stop the activity if pain is felt in the muscle group being worked.
9. Ensure that there is adequate rest between sets, especially when maximum loadings are being used.
10. Further intensive work should not immediately follow strength training because there will be a high risk of damage to soft and connective tissues.

It is not my intention to cover all aspects of technique associated with the exercises identified in the following programmes; there are many superb publications which already cover that. However, there is a vital skill element in the safe execution of any lifting or strengthening activity and it is this, perhaps, that deters both coaches and students. They may feel that they just cannot afford the time to learn skills which they see as incidental to their sport. There is certainly some justification for believing that such time would be better spent in activities more directly related to their discipline. It is perhaps this unwillingness to learn the vital skill elements which has given rise to the aversion to weight training. However, this need no longer be the case. An increase in the number of local sports centres and health clubs has meant that guidance is now more available. Perhaps equally as important, the use of multi-gyms has reduced the risk of injury to negligible levels.

My rule of thumb is to use what are called 'captive weights' as much as possible in the early stages. There are two reasons for this. The first is that they require little or no skill to use, so the possibility of injury is reduced. The second is that they allow for the development of a general level of strength prior to using free weights. It may well be that for most students, the multi-gym covers the range of exercises required for a balanced programme. However, they might benefit more from specific exercises which are only possible using free weights.

To sum up, I would say that there are those who laud the advantage of free, as opposed to captive weights, and vice versa. I believe that neither is superior; rather, that each has its own merit. Having said that though, there does seem to be a natural progression from captive to free weights as strength, skill and confidence levels increase in both student and coach.

In the training schedules which follow, I would advise student and coach to perform each particular activity with captive weights. With a little imagination and lateral thinking, most multi-gyms will be perfectly adequate. Later on in the programme, free weight practice may perhaps be introduced, but in this case only light loads should be used.

Progressive Resistance Training

Weight training has its own jargon, and as far as the coach and student are concerned, the following expressions must be understood:

Repetitions This is the number of times a movement is repeated.

Sets This is the number of repetitions in a continuous bout of activity.

Systems This refers to different combinations of sets and repetitions. For example, '3 × 8 Bicep Curls' means three sets of eight repetitions of the exercise known as 'Bicep Curls'.

With any systematic and progressive form of training, it must be possible to assess the actual load which the student is working against. The load is critical, as are the number of repetitions and sets performed during a training unit. The student and coach must therefore distinguish clearly between the repetition of strength, as opposed to its single manifestation. Consider the following:

Perceived possible effort	Load (%)	Number of repetitions possible
maximum	100	1
sub-maximum	95	2–3
very difficult	85	4–6
difficult	75	7–10
hard	65	11–15
moderate	55	16–20
easy	45	21–30
very easy	35	31+

If the strength requirement of a martial art discipline is a single, maximal effort, then the training load must be geared accordingly. Alternatively, if the need is for constant repetition of an action, or for repeated activity, then both percentage load and the number of repetitions must be decided.

Notes on the Programmes

Schedule One

Schedule One is a general strength programme. Each of the exercises suggested consists of three sets of eight repetitions, though selecting the initial weight is a matter of trial and error. At first it is better to err on the side of caution and use light loadings. Load should be increased accordingly as strength levels improve, and it should always be such as to allow the completion of all sets and repetitions. Aim to reach 70 – 75% of maximum loading.

Schedule Two

Schedule Two is a strength endurance session. Using the trial-and-error method, a weight is selected which just allows the student to perform 15 repetitions of the exercise. Each exercise has only ONE set! As the session is repeated over succeeding weeks the student might manage 16 or more repetitions, and once he can complete 20, then the weight should be increased until he can only manage 15 repetitions. This process should be repeated each time the student achieves 20 repetitions.

Schedule Three

Schedule Three is the gross strength session. It uses fewer repetitions and consequently higher loadings, and after a cautious start of light loadings, an eventual target of up to 80% of maximum may be set.

I identify four main types of exercises when devising these or any other strengthening programmes. These are exercises which have a major effect on the:

- arms and upper body,
- abdominal muscles,
- legs; or
- general exercises which involve the whole body.

In a general routine I would recommend performing perhaps eight exercises, taking two from each group. I would also suggest following the above order. Therefore an arm exercise would be followed by an abdominal, and so on. A different exercise is used each time the sequence is repeated. This system allows each group of muscles to recover before it is used again.

Table 1 The Programmes

Name ______________________ **Height** ________ **Weight** ________

SCHEDULE 1		LOAD						
Behind Neck Press	3×8							
Bent Leg Sit-Ups	3×15							
Bicep Curls	3×8							
Leg Press	3×8							
Bench Press	3×8							
Inclined Sit-Ups	3×15							
French Press	3×8							
Half Squat	3×8							
SCHEDULE 2								
Bench Press	15–20							
Bent Leg Sit-Ups	15–20							
Straddle Dead Lift	15–20							
Leg Press	15–20							
Military Press	15–20							
Body Curls	15–20							
Hack Lift	15–20							
Half Squat	15–20							
Upright Rowing	15–20							
'V' Sits	15–20							
Split Squats	15–20							
Cleans	15–20							
Behind Neck Press	15–20							
Inclined Sit-Ups	15–20							
Jump Squats	15–20							
SCHEDULE 3								
Bench Press	3×6							
Body Curls	3×15							
Straddle Dead Lift	3×6							
Half Squat	3×6							
Military Press	3×6							
'V' Sits	3×15							
Hack Lift	3×6							
Leg Press	3×6							

Behind Neck Press

Bent Leg Sit-Ups

Bicep Curls

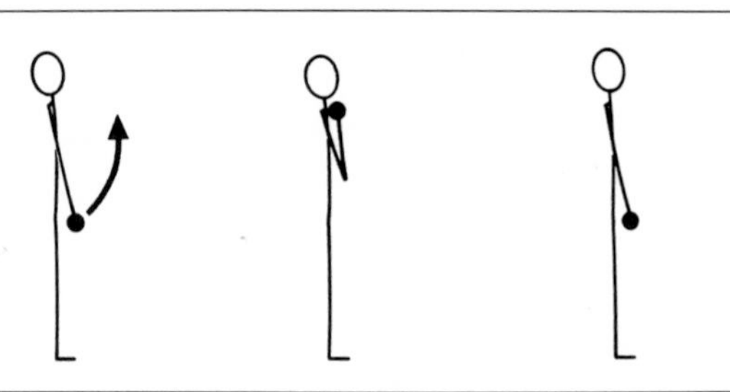

Leg Press

Bench Press

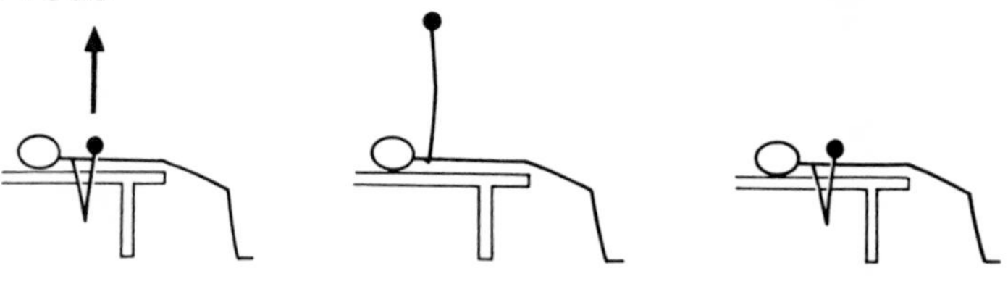

Inclined Sit-Ups

French Press

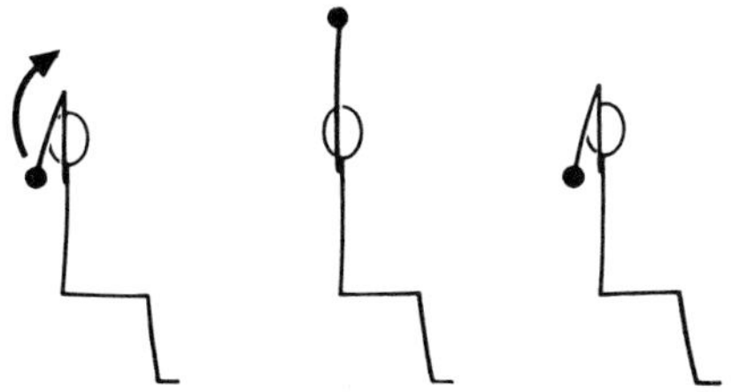

Half Squat

Body Curls

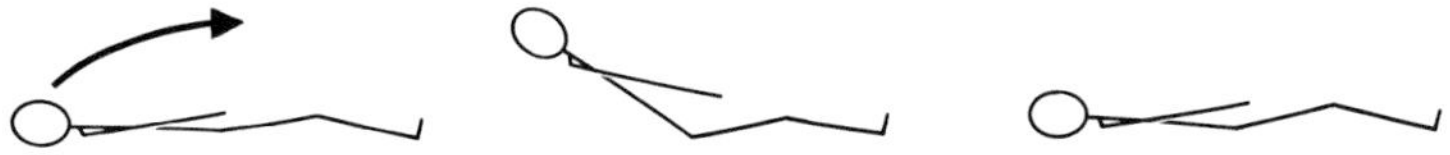

Straddle Dead Lift

Military Press

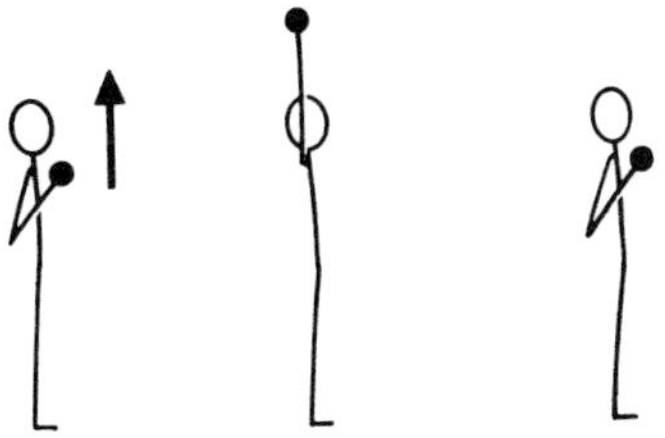

'V' Sits

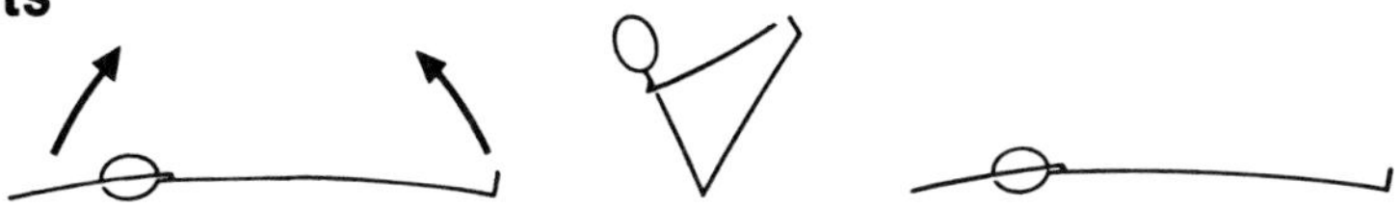

Hack Lift

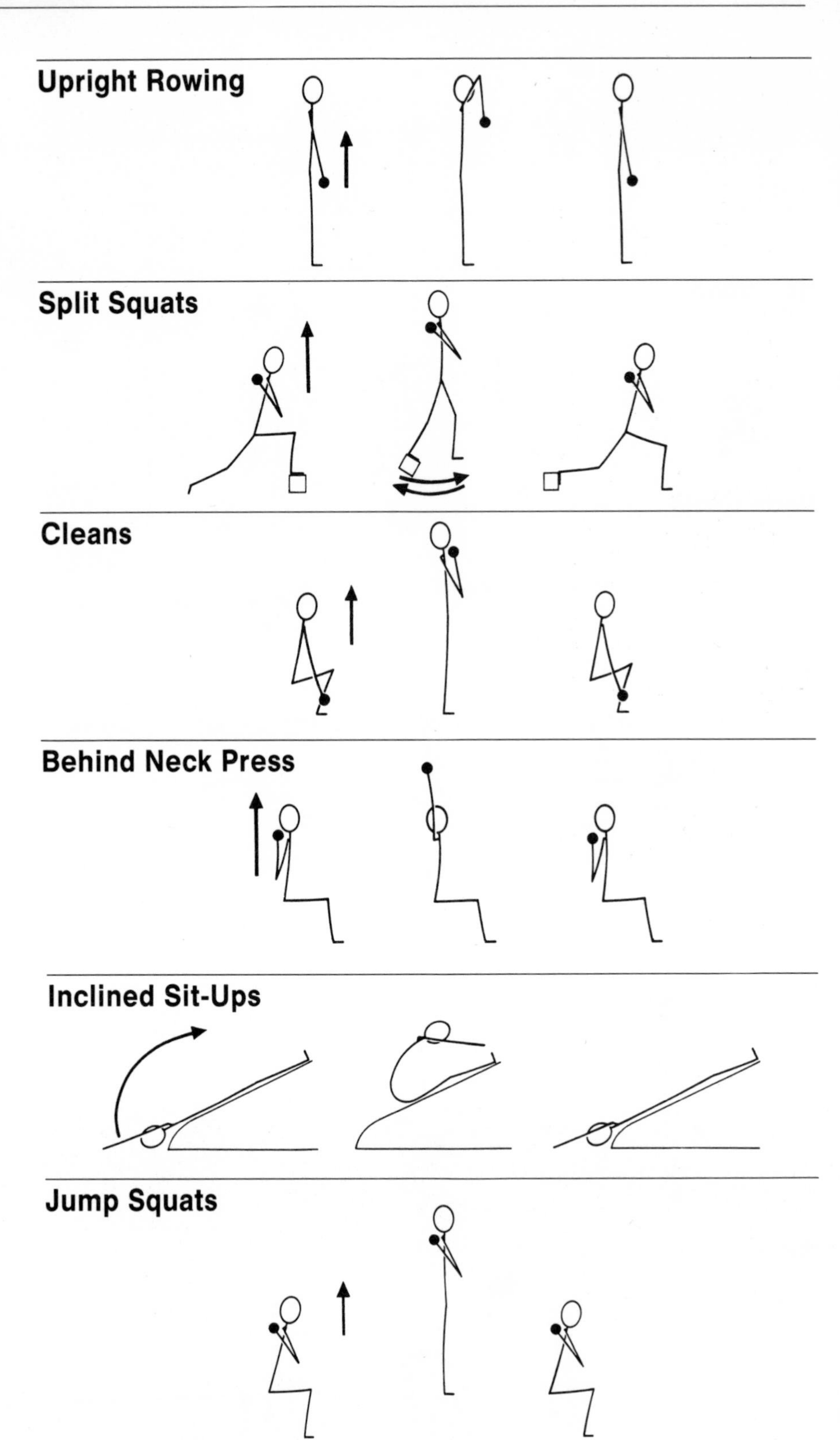
Upright Rowing
Split Squats
Cleans
Behind Neck Press
Inclined Sit-Ups
Jump Squats

Table 2 Further Strengthening Exercises

Name ______________________________ **Height** ________ **Weight** ________

EXERCISE	3×3	3×6	3×8	3×10	15–20	30 seconds	Pyramid	Personal best lift
Upper Body								
Bench Press	. . . .	. . . .	. . . .	. . . .	. . . .	. . . .	. . . .	. . . .
Inclined Press	. . . .	. . . .	. . . .	. . . .	. . . .	. . . .	. . . .	. . . .
Military Press	. . . .	. . . .	. . . .	. . . .	. . . .	. . . .	. . . .	. . . .
Behind Neck Press	. . . .	. . . .	. . . .	. . . .	. . . .	. . . .	. . . .	. . . .
Neider Press	. . . .	. . . .	. . . .	. . . .	. . . .	. . . .	. . . .	. . . .
Upright Rowing	. . . .	. . . .	. . . .	. . . .	. . . .	. . . .	. . . .	. . . .
Bent Over Rowing	. . . .	. . . .	. . . .	. . . .	. . . .	. . . .	. . . .	. . . .
Front Lats	. . . .	. . . .	. . . .	. . . .	. . . .	. . . .	. . . .	. . . .
Rear Lats	. . . .	. . . .	. . . .	. . . .	. . . .	. . . .	. . . .	. . . .
French Press	. . . .	. . . .	. . . .	. . . .	. . . .	. . . .	. . . .	. . . .
Bicep Curls	. . . .	. . . .	. . . .	. . . .	. . . .	. . . .	. . . .	. . . .
Reverse Curls	. . . .	. . . .	. . . .	. . . .	. . . .	. . . .	. . . .	. . . .
Meditation Curls	. . . .	. . . .	. . . .	. . . .	. . . .	. . . .	. . . .	. . . .
B/Arm Pulloversift	. . . .	. . . .	. . . .	. . . .	. . . .	. . . .	. . . .	. . . .
S/Arm Pullovers	. . . .	. . . .	. . . .	. . . .	. . . .	. . . .	. . . .	. . . .
Flying	. . . .	. . . .	. . . .	. . . .	. . . .	. . . .	. . . .	. . . .
Lateral Raises	. . . .	. . . .	. . . .	. . . .	. . . .	. . . .	. . . .	. . . .
A/Dumbell Press	. . . .	. . . .	. . . .	. . . .	. . . .	. . . .	. . . .	. . . .
Reverse Flying	. . . .	. . . .	. . . .	. . . .	. . . .	. . . .	. . . .	. . . .
Dumbell Punching	. . . .	. . . .	. . . .	. . . .	. . . .	. . . .	. . . .	. . . .
Abdominals								
Body Curls	. . . .	. . . .	. . . .	. . . .	. . . .	. . . .	. . . .	. . . .
D/L Circling	. . . .	. . . .	. . . .	. . . .	. . . .	. . . .	. . . .	. . . .
S/L Circling	. . . .	. . . .	. . . .	. . . .	. . . .	. . . .	. . . .	. . . .
Bent Leg Sit-Ups	. . . .	. . . .	. . . .	. . . .	. . . .	. . . .	. . . .	. . . .
'V' Sit-Ups	. . . .	. . . .	. . . .	. . . .	. . . .	. . . .	. . . .	. . . .
Inclined Sit-Ups	. . . .	. . . .	. . . .	. . . .	. . . .	. . . .	. . . .	. . . .
Leg Press	. . . .	. . . .	. . . .	. . . .	. . . .	. . . .	. . . .	. . . .
Ski Sit	. . . .	. . . .	. . . .	. . . .	. . . .	. . . .	. . . .	. . . .
Trunk Twisters	. . . .	. . . .	. . . .	. . . .	. . . .	. . . .	. . . .	. . . .
Scissors	. . . .	. . . .	. . . .	. . . .	. . . .	. . . .	. . . .	. . . .
GENERAL								
Power Clean & Jerk	. . . .	. . . .	. . . .	. . . .	. . . .	. . . .	. . . .	. . . .
Snatch	. . . .	. . . .	. . . .	. . . .	. . . .	. . . .	. . . .	. . . .
Dead Lift	. . . .	. . . .	. . . .	. . . .	. . . .	. . . .	. . . .	. . . .
Straddle Dead Lift	. . . .	. . . .	. . . .	. . . .	. . . .	. . . .	. . . .	. . . .

Table 2 *(continued)*

EXERCISE	3×3	3×6	3×8	3×10	15–20	30 seconds	Pyramid	Personal best lift
Bench Dead Lift	....	....	....	....	....	....	....	....
High Dead Lift	....	....	....	....	....	....	....	....
Hack Lift	....	....	....	....	....	....	....	....
Hip Cleans	....	....	....	....	....	....	....	....
LEGS								
Leg Press	....	....	....	....	....	....	....	....
Half Squat	....	....	....	....	....	....	....	....
Front Squat	....	....	....	....	....	....	....	....
Jump Squat	....	....	....	....	....	....	....	....
Split Squat	....	....	....	....	....	....	....	....
Calf Raises	....	....	....	....	....	....	....	....
Quad Raises	....	....	....	....	....	....	....	....
Hamstring Curls	....	....	....	....	....	....	....	....
Step-Ups	....	....	....	....	....	....	....	....

Advanced Weight Training

The schedules I have suggested are very general and serve only as examples of what can be done. I have used them as introductory programmes, to be practised as single units, or as part of a programme such as the following:

Monday	Schedule One
Wednesday	Schedule Two
Friday	Schedule Three

These will provide a good basis for moving on to more advanced programmes which are highly specific to the needs of both the activity and the student. To allow you to customise the individual training programme, I have devised a list of typical exercises which are divided into my four main groups (arms and upper body, abdominals, legs and general.) This list is by no means exhaustive but it will allow you to select exercises which are more appropriate to your needs. Further exercises are given in the many books available on this subject.

Different systems may be used even in the same training session. For example:

			Percentage of Maximum Load
Bench Press	(arms)	3 × 3	95%
Bent Leg Sit-Ups	(abdominals)	3 × 20	55%
Power Cleans	(general)	3 × 6	85%
Half Squat	(legs)	3 × 10	75%
Military Press	(arms)	5–4–3–2–1 (increase weight as repetitions decrease)	85%–90%–95%–100%
Inclined Sit-Ups	(abdominals)	3 × 10	75%
Hack Lift	(general)	3 × 4	85%
Calf Raises	(legs)	3 × 15	65%

The above is designed for gross strength but a similar session could be devised for strength endurance by either using more repetitions or by working over a given period of time (say 30 seconds). The various columns are for the student or coach to keep a careful record of loads and how they increase with systematic training. Accurate records must be kept so progess can be monitored.

Strength Training Without Equipment

The use of sophisticated weight training equipment is very beneficial in the development of strength. As I have shown, the specific type of strength required can be isolated and developed by manipulating the load, the number of repetitions and the sets of repetitions. However, similar improvements in strength can be obtained without using equipment, though a little imagination and forethought is required. The following is an example of a programme designed to work the four areas of the body previously identified.

Before describing the programme, I would like to point out that since the load is the student's own body, the types of strength developed are:

- Relative Strength,
- Strength Endurance,
- Local Muscular Endurance.

Initially, the load is increased by raising the number of repetitions and/or sets but it can also be increased dramatically by using imagination and manipulation, so gross forms of strength development can be achieved as well. I shall have more to say about this shortly.

Press-ups (narrow)

Fig. 1 The starting position for a narrow press-up

Fig. 2 Note the position of the hands, index fingers and thumbs touching. The nose goes into the triangle they form

Split squats

Fig. 3 The starting position for a split squat

Fig. 4 Jump as high as possible, changing the position of the feet while airborne prior to landing . . .

Fig. 5 . . . using both arms to help control the impact

Burpees

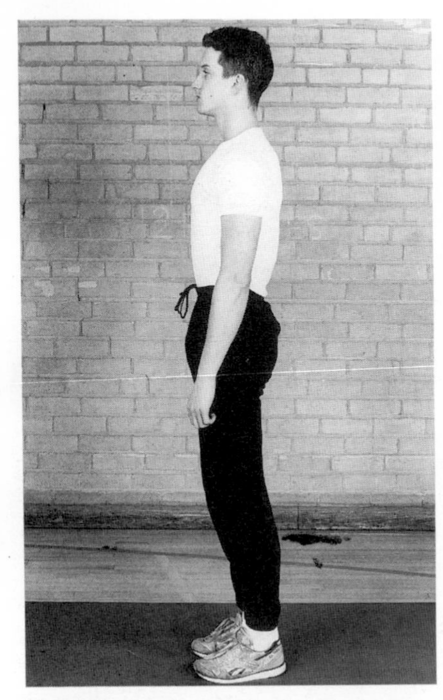

Fig. 6 The starting position for a burpee

Fig. 7 Drop to a squatting position . . .

Fig. 8 . . . extend the legs backwards . . .

Fig. 9 . . . draw legs back to squat position

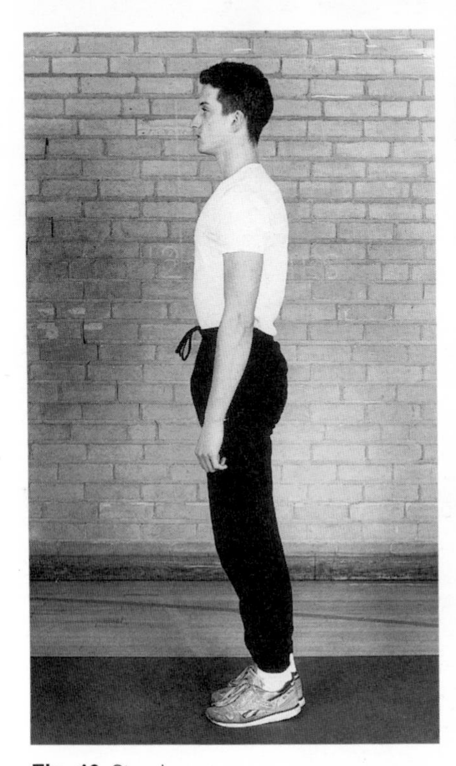

Fig. 10 Stand

Body Curls

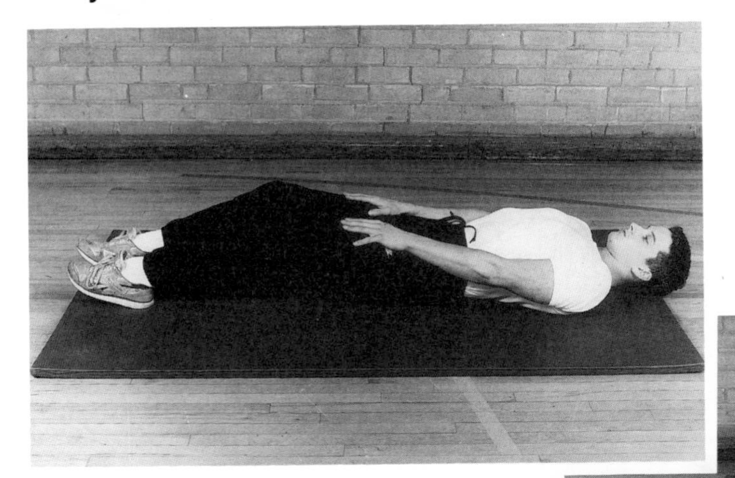

Fig. 11 The starting position for a body curl. Note that the knees are slightly bent

Fig. 12 Slide the hands forwards until they just touch the knees, then lower the shoulders back to the floor

Press-ups (extended)

Fig. 13 The starting position for an extended press-up

Fig. 14 The hands should be as wide as possible

Jump squats

Fig. 15 The starting position for jump squats

Fig. 16 Jump as high as possible, lifting the knees as close to the chest as possible

Wrestlers' Press-ups

Fig. 17 The starting position for a wrestler's press-up

Fig. 18 Lower the shoulders until the nose just touches the floor . . .

Fig. 19 . . . push the nose along the floor as far as possible . . .

Fig. 20 . . . then lift the shoulders and arch the back . . .

Fig. 21 . . . before raising the hips into the starting position

Bent Leg Sit-ups

Fig. 22 The starting position for bent leg sit-ups. Note that the knees are bent to about 90 degrees

Fig. 23 Rather undignified, the feet should be at least shoulder width apart

Fig. 24 Sit up until the elbows just touch the knees

Hand Clap Press-ups

Fig. 25 The starting position for a hand clap press-up. Hands shoulder width apart

Fig. 26 Lower chest to the floor keeping tension in the muscles of the shoulders and arms . . .

Fig. 27 . . . as soon as the chest touches the floor push up vigorously to allow for the hands to be brought together. The harder the push, the more height, the more time to clap hands

Ski Sit

Fig. 28 The ski sit. Head, shoulders and back flat against the wall. Arms folded. Knees bent to 90 degrees

The No-Equipment Strength Training Programme

Exercise	A	B	C	D	E
Press-ups (narrow)	30	25	15	10	5
Split Squats	30	25	15	10	5
Burpees	12	10	8	6	4
Body Curls	30	25	15	10	8
Press-ups (extended)	15	10	6	4	3
Jump Squats	30	25	15	10	5
Wrestlers' Press-ups	20	15	10	8	6
Bent Leg Sit-ups	30	25	15	10	8
Hand Clap Press-ups	15	10	6	4	3
Ski Sit (time in seconds)	90	75	45	30	15

The student and coach can adapt the above programme in many ways, depending on needs and the initial level of strength. The following examples illustrate how such a programme might be adapted:
1 × E might be used as part of a warm up.
2 × D might be sufficient for a novice student.
3 × C might be the normal programme for an average student.

I would aim to develop the student's strength so he can work three times through the routine without a break! To vary the activity, the coach might say to an individual 'Do 1 × A, then 1 × C and finish with 1 × E to warm down'. How the training load is varied to meet the needs of the student and to keep it fresh and enjoyable is one of the essential elements of good coaching.

As I mentioned earlier, the training load can be modified in a variety of ways. For example, Press-ups can be made more difficult by raising the feet and by this means, putting more load on the hands. Put the feet on a bench, chair, or a partner's back! The higher the feet, the greater the loading until eventually they become 'Handstand Press-ups', with the feet resting against the wall or being supported by a partner. A partner can offer variable resistance by pushing down (carefully!) on the shoulders during press-ups. The more weight that is applied, the harder it becomes!

A partner can also make abdominal exercises harder. During sit-ups, for example, he can provide a variable resistance by straddling your legs and placing his hands against your chest or arms. Jump Squats can be modified by the partner standing behind you with his hands resting on the shoulders and pushing down. In fact most exercises can be modified so that most if not all of the specific strength requirements can be attained without recourse to equipment.

Strength Training Variations on a Theme

Perhaps one of the more traditional types of strength training is that which uses gymnasium equipment such as:

wallbars	rope ladders
vaulting boxes	benches
parallel bars	beams
climbing ropes	high bars

With these, an imaginative coach can design both an interesting and a demanding programme to develop particular parts of the body in a specific way. This type of activity is sometimes called 'circuit training', because the student works at each exercise and then goes to the next, and so on for a series of circuits. Circuit training is too often seen as being only suitable for developing strength endurance, because it typically involves light loads/high repetitions. This need not, however, be the case and more absolute forms of strength can be developed by:

- increasing the load,
- modifying the activity slightly,
- using a partner to increase resistance.

Plyometrics

The theory of plyometrics is quite simple. If a muscle is already stretched and under tension, then when it does contract, it does so much more quickly than normal. It helps to visualise a piece of elastic. If it is already stretched, then it will contract faster. The force generated might well be the same but it is produced over a much shorter period. You can see why plyometrics is sometimes called 'elastic strength'! Knowledge of plyometrics is therefore useful for speed/power production and though at first it may seem an odd notion, it is nevertheless a fact that most fast or powerful movements depend on it. For example, the hips which initiate a punching technique move ahead of the trunk and stretch the muscles. Then the trunk muscles move ahead of the shoulders, stretching those muscles too. The shoulders move ahead of the arms and cause a final contraction as the punch is delivered.

Therefore what we have is a series of movements, each of which stretches the next group of muscles to be used, and the result is a powerful movement. Practising the technique at speed will help develop plyometric strength, but it can also be developed in a series of interesting and fun-type activities.

The load to use is generally that of bodyweight alone. Additional loads can be used but they must be light! In fact the East Germans recommend that in order to develop speed of movement/power, loads should not exceed 5 – 10% of maximum. If more than that is used, then a different aspect of strength will be developed.

For the purposes of plyometric training, I have once again divided the body into four areas. Just to remind you, these are:

- arms and upper body,
- abdominal muscles,
- legs,
- the whole body.

Arms and Upper body

Fig. 29 The sit up and throw. Laying on the back, knees slightly bent both arms above the head holding the medicine ball

Fig. 30 Sit up trying to keep the medicine ball behind the head . . .

Fig. 31 (right) . . . keeping the upper body moving forward, complete the action by throwing the medicine ball forward to an attentive partner!

Legs

Fig. 32 Double leg kick. Laying on the back raise both feet off the floor, knees bent, to . . .

Fig. 33 . . . kick a carefully thrown medicine ball back to a partner

Fig. 34 Single leg kick. Laying on the back raise the right foot off the floor, knee bent, and . . .

Fig. 35 . . . kick the medicine ball back to a partner. The left leg can be used in exactly the same way

Fig. 36 Hamstring curls. Laying on the front legs straight, feet together. A partner rolls the medicine ball along the back of the legs . . .

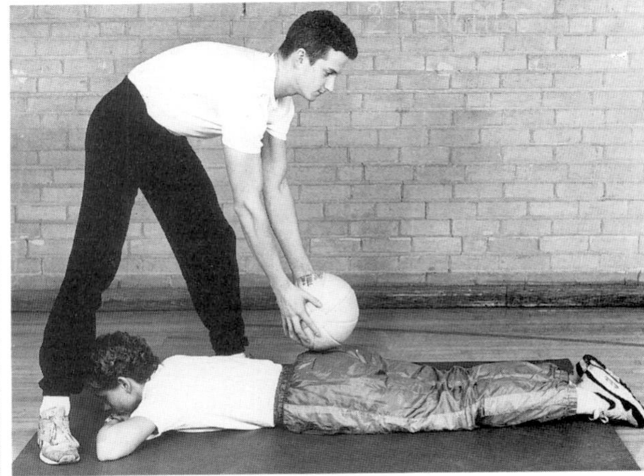

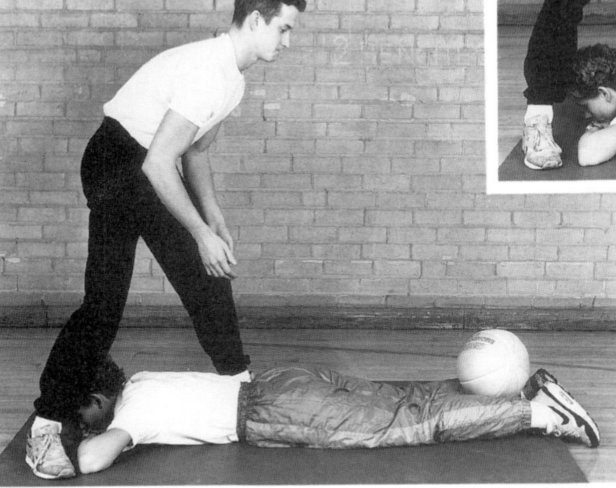

Fig. 37 . . . down to the back of the ankles, when . . .

Fig. 38 . . . the knees are bent quickly, to . . .

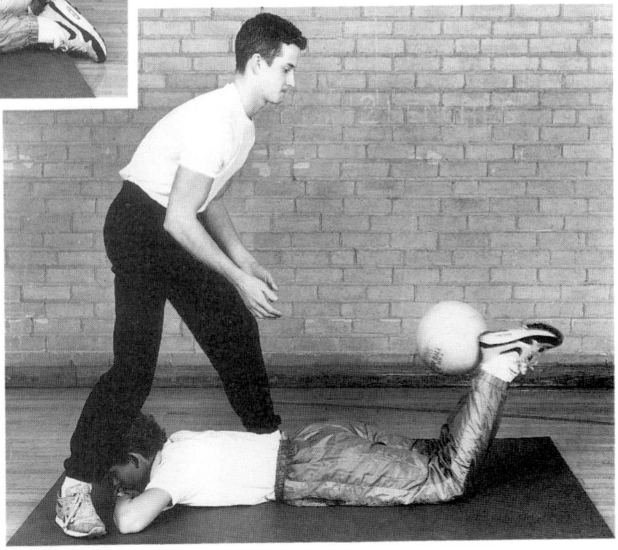

Fig. 39 . . . flick the ball back to a partner

Fig. 40 Knee drive. The partner throws the medicine ball such that it can be 'kneed' back to him/her

Fig. 41 Kick the medicine ball back towards a partner. Punch the medicine ball back towards a partner

Fig. 42 Pick up and throw. For a right-handed student, left foot forward towards the direction of throw, the medicine ball by the side of the right foot. Bend down to pick up the medicine ball . . .

Fig. 43 . . . in one flowing action pick up the ball, drive the right hip, trunk and shoulders towards the front . . .

Fig. 44 . . . releasing the medicine ball high over the left foot

Fig. 45 Under and over. Back to back with a partner, feet apart. Bend down to pass the ball backwards through the legs . . .

Fig. 46 . . . which is then lifted up overhead to be taken and the whole action repeated. The direction of the action can be reversed

Fig. 47 Roundabouts. Sitting back to back, arms straight holding the medicine ball turn . . .

Fig. 48 . . . to pass the ball to the partner . . .

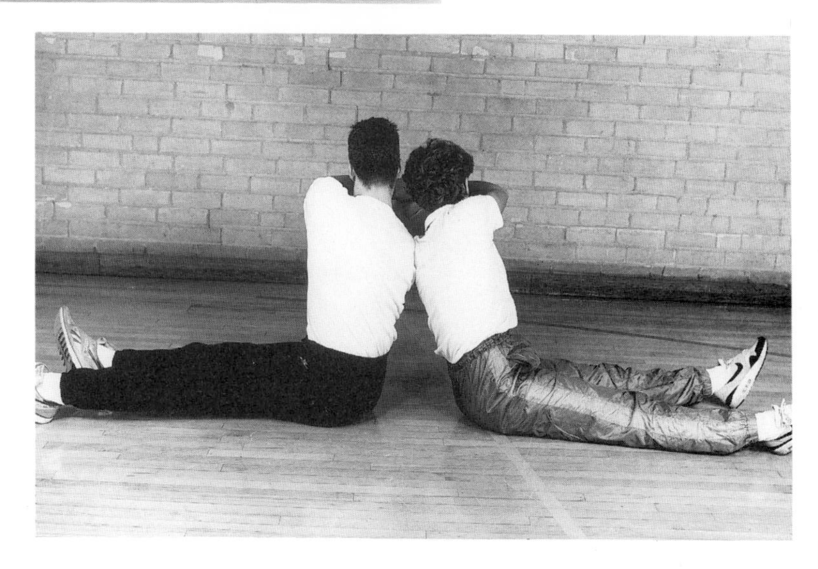

Fig. 49 . . . who keeps the ball moving in the same direction and repeats the action. The ball can be passed in both directions

It wasn't so long ago that medicine balls were much used in many gymnasia and from the plyometrics point of view, it is interesting to note that a medicine ball fits very nicely into the required 5–10% loading. This particular training aide can be used to develop plyometric strength in the arms and upper body through a whole range of activities based on catching, throwing and pushing actions. The astute coach must identify those which best mirror the particular movement pattern required and if none do, then he must modify one until it does.

The 'Throwing Decathlon' training aid has been developed at Carnegie College by Wilf Paish. This incorporates ten activities which can either be practised as activities in their own right, or they can be used to assess shoulder power/speed. Plyometric training for the legs is based upon a whole range of jumping activities, including hops, steps and jumps on and off, or over platforms of different heights. Wilf's 'Jumping Decathlon' sets out an excellent training regime based upon a whole series of jumping and bounding activities which are performed at speed. Whole-body plyometric exercises are possibly the most useful for martial artists and I recommend using a medicine ball to reproduce a movement pattern.

The Throwing Decathlon

Measure from the 'scratch' line or from the frontmost part of the body, i.e. the toes, heels or head, to the point where the medicine ball lands. Record the best of three attempts and score as before. At any one time select only 3–5 activities.

Using the Throwing Decathlon Tables

Having decided which events you are going to test your students on, record the best of three efforts. Suppose it was the Push from Chest and the best distance achieved was 10.20 m. Find the column for the activity and go down it until you find 10.20. Read off the score in the left-hand column, which in this case is 51 points. Repeat this procedure for the other events. Should the distance thrown not coincide with the appropriate table, for example in the Caber Throw where a student records a best of 16.61, go to the nearest figure below, which in this case is 16.50, and read off the score (66 points).

Table 3 The Throwing Decathlon

	1 Overhead double-handed throw	2 Kneeling putt dominant arm	3 Throw through legs	4 Standing discus	5 Hammer style throw	6 Football throw-in style	7 Push from chest	8 Caber throw	9 Kneeling non-dominant arm	10 Back lying overhead throw
100	22.00	14.00	6.00	30.00	30.00	20.00	20.00	25.00	12.00	10.00
99	21.78	13.86	5.94	29.70	29.70	19.80	19.80	24.75	11.88	9.90
98	21.56	13.72	5.88	29.40	29.40	19.60	19.60	24.50	11.76	9.80
97	21.34	13.58	5.82	29.10	29.10	19.40	19.40	24.25	11.64	9.70
96	21.12	13.44	5.76	28.80	28.80	19.20	19.20	24.00	11.52	9.60
95	20.90	13.30	5.70	28.50	28.50	19.00	19.00	23.75	11.40	9.50
94	20.68	13.16	5.64	28.20	28.20	18.80	18.80	23.50	11.28	9.40
93	20.46	13.02	5.58	27.90	27.90	18.60	18.60	23.25	11.16	9.30
92	20.24	12.88	5.52	27.60	27.60	18.40	18.40	23.00	11.04	9.20
91	20.02	12.74	5.46	27.30	27.30	18.20	18.20	22.75	10.92	9.10
90	19.80	12.60	5.40	27.00	27.00	18.00	18.00	22.50	10.80	9.00
89	19.58	12.46	5.34	26.70	26.70	17.80	17.80	22.25	10.68	8.90
88	19.36	12.32	5.28	26.40	26.40	17.60	17.60	22.00	10.56	8.80
87	19.14	12.18	5.22	26.10	26.10	17.40	17.40	21.75	10.44	8.70
86	18.92	12.04	5.16	25.80	25.80	17.20	17.20	21.50	10.32	8.60
85	18.70	11.90	5.10	25.50	25.50	17.00	17.00	21.25	10.20	8.50
84	18.48	11.76	5.04	25.20	25.20	16.80	16.80	21.00	10.00	8.40
83	18.26	11.62	4.98	24.90	24.90	16.60	16.60	20.75	9.96	8.30
82	18.04	11.48	4.92	24.60	24.60	16.40	16.40	20.50	9.84	8.20
81	17.82	11.34	4.86	24.30	24.30	16.20	16.20	20.25	9.72	8.10
80	17.60	11.20	4.80	24.00	24.00	16.00	16.00	20.00	9.60	8.00
79	17.38	11.06	4.74	23.70	23.70	15.80	15.80	19.75	9.48	7.90
78	17.16	10.92	4.68	23.40	23.40	15.60	15.60	19.50	9.36	7.80
77	16.94	10.78	4.62	23.10	23.10	15.40	15.40	19.25	9.24	7.70
76	16.72	10.64	4.56	22.80	22.80	15.20	15.20	19.00	9.12	7.60
75	16.50	10.50	4.50	22.50	22.50	15.00	15.00	18.75	9.00	7.50
74	16.28	10.36	4.44	22.20	22.20	14.80	14.80	18.50	8.88	7.40
73	16.06	10.22	4.38	21.90	21.90	14.60	14.60	18.25	8.76	7.30
72	15.84	10.08	4.32	21.60	21.60	14.40	14.40	18.00	8.64	7.20
71	15.62	9.94	4.25	21.30	21.30	14.20	14.20	17.75	8.52	7.10
70	15.40	9.80	4.20	21.00	21.00	14.00	14.00	17.50	8.40	7.00
69	15.18	9.66	4.14	20.70	20.70	13.80	13.80	17.25	8.28	6.90
68	14.96	9.52	4.08	20.40	20.40	13.60	13.60	17.00	2.16	6.80
67	14.74	9.38	4.02	20.10	20.10	13.40	13.40	16.75	8.04	6.70
66	14.52	9.24	3.96	19.80	19.80	13.20	13.20	16.50	7.92	6.60
65	14.30	9.10	3.90	19.50	19.50	13.00	13.00	16.25	7.80	6.50
64	14.08	8.96	3.84	19.20	19.20	12.80	12.80	16.00	7.68	6.40
63	13.86	8.82	3.78	18.90	18.90	12.60	12.60	15.75	7.56	6.30
62	13.64	8.68	3.72	18.60	18.60	12.40	12.40	15.50	7.44	6.20
61	13.42	8.54	3.66	18.30	18.30	12.20	12.26	15.25	7.32	6.10
60	13.20	8.40	3.60	18.00	18.00	12.00	12.00	15.00	7.20	6.00
59	12.98	8.26	3.54	17.70	17.70	11.80	11.80	14.75	7.08	5.90
58	12.76	8.12	3.48	17.40	17.40	11.60	11.60	14.50	6.96	5.80
57	12.54	7.98	3.42	17.10	17.10	11.40	11.40	14.25	6.84	5.70
56	12.32	7.84	3.36	16.80	16.80	11.20	11.20	14.00	6.72	5.60
55	12.10	7.70	3.30	16.50	16.50	11.00	11.00	13.75	6.60	5.50
54	11.88	7.56	3.24	16.20	16.20	10.80	10.80	13.50	6.48	5.40
53	11.66	7.42	3.18	15.90	15.90	10.60	10.60	13.25	6.36	5.30
52	11.44	7.28	3.12	15.60	15.60	10.40	10.40	13.00	6.24	5.20
51	11.22	7.14	3.06	15.30	15.30	10.20	10.20	12.75	6.12	5.10
50	11.00	7.00	3.00	15.00	15.00	10.00	10.00	12.50	6.00	5.00

	1	2	3	4	5	6	7	8	9	10
49	10.78	6.86	2.94	14.70	14.70	9.80	9.80	12.25	5.88	4.90
48	10.56	6.72	2.88	14.40	14.40	9.60	9.60	12.00	5.76	4.80
47	10.34	6.58	2.82	14.10	14.10	9.40	9.40	11.75	5.64	4.70
46	10.12	6.44	2.76	13.80	13.80	9.20	9.20	11.50	5.52	4.60
45	9.90	6.30	2.70	13.50	13.50	9.00	9.00	11.25	5.40	4.50
44	9.68	6.16	2.64	13.20	13.20	8.80	8.80	11.00	5.28	4.40
43	9.46	6.02	2.58	12.90	12.90	8.60	8.60	10.75	5.16	4.30
42	9.24	5.88	2.52	12.60	12.60	8.40	8.40	10.50	5.04	4.20
41	9.02	5.74	2.46	12.30	12.30	8.20	8.20	10.25	4.92	4.10
40	8.80	5.60	2.40	12.00	12.00	8.00	8.00	10.00	4.80	4.00
39	8.58	5.46	2.34	11.80	11.70	7.80	7.80	9.75	4.68	3.90
38	8.36	5.32	2.28	11.40	11.40	7.60	7.60	9.50	4.56	3.80
37	8.14	5.18	2.22	11.10	11.10	7.40	7.40	9.25	4.48	3.70
36	7.92	5.04	2.16	10.80	10.80	7.20	7.20	9.00	4.32	3.60
35	7.70	4.90	2.10	10.50	10.50	7.00	7.00	8.75	4.20	3.50
34	7.48	4.76	2.04	10.20	10.20	6.80	6.80	8.50	4.08	3.40
33	7.26	4.62	1.98	9.90	9.90	6.60	6.60	8.25	3.96	3.30
32	7.04	4.48	1.92	9.60	9.60	6.40	6.40	8.00	3.84	3.20
31	6.82	4.34	1.86	9.30	9.30	6.20	6.20	7.55	3.72	3.10
30	6.60	4.20	1.80	9.00	9.00	6.00	6.00	7.50	3.60	3.00
29	6.38	4.06	1.74	8.70	8.70	5.80	5.80	7.25	3.48	2.90
28	6.16	3.92	1.68	8.40	8.40	5.60	5.60	7.00	3.36	2.80
27	5.94	3.78	1.62	8.10	8.10	5.40	5.40	6.75	3.24	2.70
26	5.72	3.64	1.56	7.80	7.80	5.20	5.20	6.50	3.12	2.60
25	5.50	3.50	1.50	7.50	7.50	5.00	5.00	6.25	3.00	2.50
24	5.28	3.36	1.44	7.20	7.20	4.80	4.80	6.00	2.88	2.40
23	5.06	3.22	1.38	6.90	6.90	4.60	4.60	5.75	2.76	2.30
22	4.84	3.08	1.32	6.60	6.60	4.40	4.40	5.50	2.64	2.20
21	4.62	2.94	1.26	6.30	6.30	4.20	4.20	5.25	2.52	2.10
20	4.40	2.80	1.20	6.00	6.00	4.00	4.00	5.00	2.40	2.00
19	4.18	2.66	1.14	5.70	5.70	3.80	3.80	4.75	2.28	1.90
18	3.96	2.52	1.08	5.40	5.40	3.60	3.60	4.50	2.16	1.80
17	3.74	2.38	1.02	5.10	5.10	3.40	3.40	4.25	2.04	1.70
16	3.52	2.24	0.96	4.80	4.80	3.20	3.20	4.00	1.92	1.60
15	3.30	2.10	0.90	4.50	4.50	3.00	3.00	3.75	1.80	1.50
14	3.08	1.96	0.84	4.20	4.20	2.80	2.80	3.50	1.68	1.40
13	2.86	1.82	0.78	3.90	3.90	2.60	2.60	3.25	1.56	1.30
12	2.64	1.68	0.72	3.60	3.60	2.40	2.40	3.00	1.44	1.20
11	2.42	1.54	0.66	3.30	3.30	2.20	2.20	2.75	1.32	1.10
10	2.20	1.40	0.60	3.00	3.00	2.00	2.00	2.50	1.20	1.00
9	1.98	1.26	0.54	2.70	2.70	1.80	1.80	2.25	1.08	0.90
8	1.76	1.12	0.48	2.40	2.40	1.60	1.60	2.00	0.96	0.80
7	1.54	0.98	0.42	2.10	2.10	1.40	1.40	1.75	0.84	0.70
6	1.32	0.84	0.36	1.80	1.80	1.20	1.20	1.50	0.72	0.60
5	1.10	0.70	0.30	1.50	1.50	1.00	1.00	1.25	0.60	0.50
4	0.88	0.56	0.24	1.20	1.20	0.80	0.80	1.00	0.48	0.40
3	0.66	0.42	0.18	0.90	0.90	0.60	0.60	0.75	0.36	0.30
2	0.44	0.28	0.12	0.60	0.60	0.40	0.40	0.50	0.24	0.20
1	0.22	0.14	0.6	0.30	0.30	0.20	0.20	0.25	0.12	0.10
0	0.00	0.00	0.00	0.00	0.00	0.00	0.00	0.00	0.00	0.00

Overhead Double-handed Throw

Fig. 50 The overhead double-handed throw. Back towards the direction of throw, bend down holding the medicine ball in both hands level with the knees

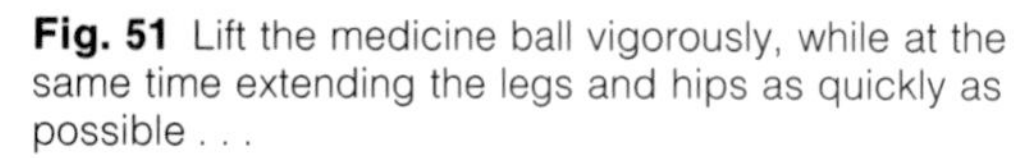

Fig. 51 Lift the medicine ball vigorously, while at the same time extending the legs and hips as quickly as possible . . .

Fig. 52 . . . continuing to lift the medicine ball up and over the head to release. Note the arch of the back on delivery

Kneeling Putt Dominant Arm

Fig. 53 The kneeling putt – dominant arm. For a right-handed student the throwing position is kneeling on the right knee, left forward. The medicine ball is held under the right ear in the right hand. The shoulders are turned away from the direction as far as possible

Fig. 54 The right shoulder is driven round and forwards with the right arm finally pushing the medicine ball away from the body

Throw through Legs

Fig. 55 The throw through the legs. Facing the direction of throw take the arms behind the legs so that the medicine ball can be held in both hands

Fig. 56 With a flick of the wrists throw the medicine ball upwards and forwards

Standing Discus Throw

Fig. 57 The standing discus throw. For a right-handed student the throwing position is left foot forward, right foot back. The body and throwing arm is turned as far as possible from the direction of throw

Fig. 58 The hips are driven round and forward followed by the trunk and arm . . .

Fig. 59 . . . releasing the medicine ball with a final fling of the arm

Hammer Style Throw

Fig. 60 The hammer style throw. For a right-handed student the throwing position is back to the direction of throw, holding the medicine ball in both hands. Turn as far away from the direction of throw as possible

Fig. 61 Drive the right hip, trunk and arms round towards the front . . .

Fig. 62 . . . lifting the arms to deliver the medicine ball high over the left shoulder

Football Throw-in Style

Fig. 63 The football throw-in style. Facing the direction of throw, for a right-handed student, left foot forward, lean back as far as possible holding the medicine ball in both hands

Fig. 64 Drive the right hip, trunk and arms forward . . .

Fig. 65 . . . to release the medicine ball high over the left foot

Push from Chest

Fig. 66 (Far left) The push from the chest. Stand facing the direction of throw the medicine ball held in both hands elbows high

Fig. 67 (Left) Vigorously extend the arms, giving the medicine ball a final flick with the wrists

Caber Throw

Fig. 68 (Far left) The caber throw. Facing the direction of throw hold the medicine ball in both hands between the knees

Fig. 69 (Left) Extend the legs, hips and arms upwards and forwards into the delivery

Kneeling Putt Non-dominant Arm

Fig. 70 The kneeling putt – non dominant arm. For a right-handed student this would require using the left arm. The throwing position is kneeling on the left knee, right foot forward. The medicine ball is held under the left ear in the left hand. The shoulders are turned as far as possible from the direction of throw

Fig. 71 The left shoulder is driven forwards with the arm finally pushing the medicine ball away from the body

Back Lying Overhead Throw

Fig. 72 Back lying overhead throw. Lying head towards the direction of throw. Hold the medicine ball in both hands resting on the legs

Fig. 73 Drive the arms upwards and backwards to release the medicine ball over the head

The Jumping Decathlon

The first of the ten activities is the Standing Long Jump, the second being the Standing Triple Jump. The other activities are combinations of Hops, Steps and Jumps, the name of each clearly describing the sequence of movements. The Five Spring Jumps are a series of five standing long jumps, one immediately following the other with no pause between. All the activities start from a standing position with the exception of the 'Run, Four Hops and a Jump', where a short run-up is allowed. Similarly with the 'Five-stride Long Jump' a controlled run-up of five strides is required before taking off. The '25-metre Hop' is a timed event on the strongest, or weakest, leg. All the other events are measured from the take-off line to the back of the heels on landing. If a student falls back on landing, measure to the nearest point to the take-off line, e.g. hands or bottom!

To work out the score, record the best of three attempts. Go down the appropriate column until the distance or time, or the nearest to it, is found. Then follow the line across to the left-hand side to obtain the score out of 100. Don't select more than three to five activities on any one occasion – more than that can become very demanding. Score in exactly the same way as for the Throwing Decathlon.

Long Jump

Fig. 74 The standing long jump. Feet about shoulder width apart. Bend the knees and take both arms behind the back. Note the feet are just behind the take-off mark

Fig. 75 At the start of the movement throw both arms forward and upwards while at the same time extending the legs

Fig. 76 Make sure that the knees bend on landing. Measure from the take-off mark to the back of the heels

Triple Jump

Fig. 77 The standing triple jump might best be described, as it used to be, as the hop, step and jump. From a standing position the selected take-off foot behind the take-off mark arms taken backwards . . . drive both arms upwards and forwards while at the same time extending the take-off leg . . .

Fig. 78 . . . landing on the same leg as was used at take-off, a hop, . . . immediately drive the free leg forward as far as possible . . .

Fig. 79 . . . to land on it, a step, . . to immediately drive the free knee forward so as to jump into the air to land knees bent with both feet together, as in the long jump

Table 4 The Jumping Decathlon

	1 Stand Long Jump	2 Stand Triple Jump	3 2 Hops Step & Jump	4 2 Hops 2 Steps & Jump	5 2 Hops 2 Steps 2 Jumps	6 Five Spring Jumps	7 Stand 4 Hops & Jump	8 Run 4 Hops & Jump	9 25-Metre Hop	10 5-Stride Long Jump
100	3.73	10.51	13.00	15.54	19.15	17.06	17.67	23.77	2.07	7.28
99	–	10.43	12.90	15.46	18.99	16.91	17.52	23.62	–	–
98	3.65	10.36	12.80	15.39	18.84	16.76	17.37	23.46	2.08	–
97	–	10.28	12.69	15.31	18.69	16.61	17.22	23.31	–	7.26
96	3.58	10.21	12.59	15.08	18.54	16.45	17.06	23.16	3.00	–
95	–	10.13	12.49	15.01	18.38	16.40	16.96	23.01	–	
94	3.50	10.05	12.39	14.88	18.23	16.25	16.86	22.85	3.01	7.23
93	–	9.98	12.29	14.78	18.08	16.15	16.76	22.70	–	–
92	3.42	9.90	12.19	14.68	17.93	16.00	16.61	22.55	3.02	–
91	–	9.82	12.09	14.57	17.77	15.84	16.45	22.35	–	7.21
90	3.35	9.75	11.98	14.47	17.62	15.79	16.35	21.99	3.03	–
89	–	9.68	11.88	14.37	17.47	15.64	16.25	21.79	–	–
88	3.27	9.60	11.78	14.27	17.32	15.54	16.15	21.64	3.04	7.18
87	–	9.52	11.68	14.17	17.17	15.39	16.00	21.48	–	–
86	3.20	9.44	11.58	14.07	17.01	15.23	15.84	21.33	3.05	–
85	–	9.37	11.48	13.96	16.91	15.18	15.74	21.18	–	7.16
84	3.12	9.29	11.37	13.66	16.76	15.03	15.64	21.03	3.06	–
83	–	9.22	11.27	13.76	16.66	14.93	15.54	20.80	3.07	7.13
82	3.04	9.14	11.17	13.66	16.50	14.83	15.44	20.65	3.08	–
81	–	9.06	11.07	13.56	16.35	14.68	15.34	20.42	3.09	7.11
80	2.97	8.99	10.97	13.46	16.20	14.57	15.23	20.26	4.00	–
79	–	8.91	10.87	13.36	16.10	14.42	15.08	20.11	4.02	7.08
78	2.89	8.83	10.76	13.25	16.00	14.32	14.93	19.96	4.03	–
77	–	6.76	10.66	13.15	15.84	14.22	14.83	19.81	4.04	7.06
76	2.81	8.68	10.56	13.05	15.69	14.07	14.73	19.58	4.05	7.03
75	–	8.61	10.46	12.95	15.54	13.96	14.63	19.43	4.06	7.01
74	2.74	8.53	10.36	12.85	15.39	13.86	14.47	19.20	4.07	6.95
73	2.69	8.45	10.26	12.75	15.23	13.71	14.32	19.04	4.08	6.90
72	2.66	8.38	10.15	12.64	15.13	13.61	14.22	18.89	4.09	6.85
71	2.64	8.30	10.05	12.49	15.03	13.51	14.12	18.74	5.00	6.80
70	2.61	8.22	9.95	12.42	14.88	13.41	14.02	18.59	5.01	6.75
69	2.59	8.15	9.85	12.34	14.73	13.25	13.86	18.44	5.02	6.70
68	2.56	8.07	9.75	12.19	14.63	13.10	13.71	18.28	5.04	6.62
67	2.53	8.00	9.65	12.09	14.47	13.00	13.61	18.13	5.05	6.55
66	2.51	7.92	9.55	11.98	14.32	12.90	13.51	17.98	5.06	6.47
65	2.48	7.84	9.44	11.88	14.22	12.80	13.41	17.75	5.07	6.40
64	2.46	7.77	9.34	11.78	14.07	12.69	13.30	17.60	5.08	6.32
63	2.43	7.69	9.24	11.68	13.96	12.59	13.20	17.37	5.09	6.24
62	2.41	7.61	9.14	11.58	13.81	12.49	13.10	17.22	6.00	6.17
61	2.38	7.54	9.04	11.48	13.71	12.34	12.95	17.06	6.01	6.09
60	2.36	7.46	8.94	11.37	13.56	12.19	12.80	16.91	6.02	6.01
59	2.33	7.39	8.83	11.27	13.41	12.03	12.64	16.76	6.03	5.94
58	2.31	7.31	8.73	11.17	13.25	11.88	12.49	16.53	6.05	5.86
57	2.28	7.23	8.63	11.07	13.10	11.78	12.39	16.38	6.06	5.79
56	2.26	7.16	8.53	10.97	12.95	11.68	12.29	16.15	6.07	5.71
55	2.23	7.03	8.45	10.87	12.60	11.58	12.19	16.00	6.08	5.63
54	2.20	7.01	8.38	10.76	12.64	11.48	12.09	15.84	6.09	5.56
53	2.18	6.93	8.30	10.66	12.49	11.37	11.98	15.69	7.00	5.48
52	2.15	6.85	8.22	10.56	12.34	11.27	11.58	15.54	7.01	5.41

	1	2	3	4	5	6	7	8	9	10
51	2.13	6.78	8.15	10.46	12.19	11.17	11.42	15.39	7.02	5.33
50	2.10	6.70	8.07	10.36	12.03	11.07	11.27	15.23	7.03	5.25
49	2.08	6.62	8.00	10.26	11.88	10.97	11.17	15.08	7.04	5.18
48	2.05	6.55	7.92	10.15	11.73	10.87	11.07	14.93	–	5.13
47	2.03	6.47	7.84	10.05	11.58	10.76	10.97	14.78	7.05	5.07
46	2.00	6.40	7.77	9.95	11.42	10.66	10.82	14.63	–	5.02
45	1.98	6.32	7.69	9.85	11.27	10.56	10.66	14.47	7.07	4.97
44	1.95	6.24	7.61	9.75	11.17	10.46	10.51	14.32	–	4.92
43	1.93	6.17	7.54	9.65	11.07	10.36	10.36	14.17	7.08	4.87
42	1.90	6.09	7.46	9.55	10.97	10.26	10.21	14.02	–	4.82
41	1.87	6.01	7.39	9.44	10.87	10.15	10.05	13.86	7.09	4.77
40	1.85	5.94	7.31	9.34	10.76	10.05	9.90	13.71	–	4.72
39	1.82	5.86	7.23	9.24	10.66	9.95	9.75	13.56	8.00	4.67
38	1.80	5.79	7.16	9.14	10.56	9.85	9.60	13.41	–	4.62
37	1.77	5.71	7.08	9.04	10.46	9.75	9.44	13.25	8.01	4.57
36	1.75	5.63	7.01	8.94	10.36	9.65	9.34	13.10	–	4.52
35	1.72	5.56	6.93	8.83	10.26	9.55	9.24	12.95	8.02	4.47
34	1.70	5.48	6.85	8.73	10.15	9.44	9.14	12.80	–	4.41
33	1.67	5.41	6.78	8.63	10.05	9.34	9.04	12.64	8.03	4.36
32	1.65	5.33	6.70	8.53	9.95	9.24	8.94	12.49	–	4.31
31	1.62	5.25	6.62	8.43	9.85	9.14	8.83	12.34	8.04	4.26
30	1.60	5.18	6.55	8.33	9.75	9.04	8.73	12.19	–	4.21
29	1.57	5.10	6.47	8.22	9.65	8.94	8.63	12.03	8.05	4.16
28	1.54	5.02	6.40	8.12	9.55	8.83	8.53	11.88	–	4.11
27	1.52	4.95	6.32	8.02	9.44	8.73	8.43	11.73	8.06	4.06
26	1.49	4.87	6.24	7.92	9.34	8.63	8.33	11.58	–	4.01
25	1.47	4.80	6.17	7.82	9.24	8.53	8.22	11.42	8.07	3.96
24	1.44	4.72	6.09	7.72	9.14	8.43	8.12	11.27	–	3.91
23	1.42	4.64	5.99	7.61	9.04	8.33	8.02	11.12		3.86
22	1.39	4.57	5.89	7.51	8.94	8.22	7.92	10.97	8.09	3.80
21	1.37	4.49	5.79	7.41	8.83	8.12	7.82	10.82	–	3.75
20	1.34	4.41	5.68	7.31	8.73	8.02	7.72	10.66	–	3.70
19	1.29	4.26	5.58	7.21	8.63	7.92	7.61	10.51	9.00	3.65
18	1.26	4.19	5.48	7.11	8.53	7.82	7.51	10.36	–	3.60
17	1.24	4.11	5.38	7.01	8.43	7.72	7.41	10.21	–	3.55
16	1.21	4.03	5.28	6.90	8.33	7.61	7.31	10.05	9.01	3.50
15	1.19	3.96	5.18	6.80	8.22	7.51	7.21	9.90	–	3.45
14	1.16	3.88	5.07	6.70	8.12	7.41	7.11	9.75	–	3.40
13	1.14	3.80	4.97	6.60	8.02	7.31	7.01	9.60	9.02	3.35
12	1.11	3.73	4.87	6.50	7.92	7.21	6.90	9.44	–	3.25
11	1.09	3.65	4.77	6.40	7.82	7.11	6.80	9.29	–	3.14
10	1.06	3.53	4.67	6.29	7.72	7.01	6.70	9.14	9.03	3.04
9	1.04	3.50	4.57	6.19	7.61	6.90	6.60	8.99	–	2.94
8	1.01	3.42	4.47	6.09	7.51	6.80	6.50	8.83	–	2.84
7	0.99	3.35	4.36	5.99	7.41	6.70	6.40	8.68	9.04	2.74
6	0.96	3.27	4.26	5.89	7.31	6.60	6.29	8.53	–	2.64
5	0.93	3.20	4.16	5.79	7.21	6.50	6.19	8.38	–	2.53
4	0.91	3.12	4.06	5.68	7.11	6.40	6.09	8.22	9.05	2.43
3	0.88	3.04	3.96	5.58	7.01	6.29	5.99	8.07	–	2.33
2	0.86	2.97	3.86	5.48	6.90	6.19	5.89	7.92	–	2.23
1	0.60	2.89	3.75	5.38	6.70	6.09	5.79	7.77	9.06	2.13

Speed

Perhaps second only to the technical requirements of the martial arts is the need for speed. However, as with the other components of fitness, this is not quite as simple as it may appear. The coach/student must first identify exactly what is meant by speed, as it is related to their own particular discipline. Speed may be defined in the following ways:

- the rate at which the whole body moves,
- the rate at which a limb moves.

Both of these aspects of speed might be expressed as one instantaneous action, or as the number of movements which can be performed in a given time. In the latter case, an element of endurance is also required. Other elements may also need to be considered in identifying the precise type of speed required. For example, movements may involve:

- direct speed, where pure speed of movement is required,
- indirect speed, where the optimum speed of movment is required to permit the maximum expression of relevant strength.

Whichever is required, speed depends upon a number of physiological and psychological factors, and these are as follows:

Muscle Fibre type The percentage of fast fibres as opposed to slow. Slow endurance-orientated fibres will have a major effect in limiting potential for fast movements.

Innervation The accurate selection of appropriate muscles and their fine regulation means a high rate of movement and/or speed of movement. This selection must be coordinated with the optimal production of strength by the muscle groups involved.

Elasticity The ability of the muscles to contract explosively, i.e., at high speed.

Energy Pathways The efficient utilisation of the anaerobic/aerobic systems to provide the energy appropriate to the intensity and duration of the activity.

Muscle Relaxability The ability of the working muscles to relax, allowing them to stretch in order to achieve the maximum/optimum range of movement.

Reactions The early and correct identification of appropriate cues, and the technical ability to execute the appropriate response. Experience gained in the training environment will affect the accurate selection of an appropriate response to a given situation.

Willpower The ability of the martial artist to concentrate on the task in hand and to generate the maximum conscious effort needed to achieve the maximum/optimum speed.

Some rather important considerations must be borne in mind when training to develop speed. The loadings imposed by speed training put maximum demands on muscles, tendons and ligaments, so the potential for injury is high. The main causes of injury are:

- overloading
- working at speed when cold
- working when tired
- insufficient SPECIFIC warm-up

It must be clearly understood that any practices which are aimed at the development of speed are specific to the technical demands of the parent style. Such demands vary with the requirement of strength, endurance and mobility, which, when taken together with range of movement at a joint, will produce movement of maximum or optimum speed.

With respect to specific speed training, the following must be considered:

Intensity All movements must be practised at 75–100% of maximum speed. The emphasis is on quality of movement at all times; technique is the paramount consideration.

Frequency No fatigue should be present during training, since optimal adaptation occurs only in a rested, non-fatigued neuromuscular system. The rest/work ratio should allow for full restoration of working capacity yet not be so long as to let the body cool.

Duration The work period should be short enough for the martial artist to work at his maximum output. The time involved, or the number of repetitions will ultimately depend upon the individual.

Before going on to develop the concept of speed as an essential part of martial art practice, it is as well to discuss a further aspect. Earlier, the notion of optimum speed was distinguished from absolute speed, insofar as the latter is sometimes so rapid that it does not always allow sufficient time for force to be applied. This illustrates a subtle difference between speed of movement alone, and speed of movement involving an extra dimension of force application. If this is misunderstood, then the student/coach may well confuse speed of movement with what is called 'power'. Power may be identified by the following equation:

$$\text{Power} = \frac{\text{strength to produce force} \times \text{range of movement}}{\text{time}}$$

In fact speed is only one of the components which make up power. Speed reaches a plateau, from which it can only be increased with difficulty. However, since very few martial artists ever attain their maximum levels of strength, then large gains in power are possible by increasing strength, while simply maintaining speed. Power can be improved in any one of three ways:

1. increase speed, while strength levels remain constant,

2. increase strength while speed remains constant,

3. increase both strength and speed.

Speed Training

The 'No Equipment' strength training programme can be adapted for use in speed training, and it will serve as an example of how the coach can modify training practice. Speed means moving the whole body, or part of it, as quickly as possible for one or a number of repetitions in a short period of time. Suppose the coach requires the student to perform as many repetitions as he can in a given time. Consider the following:

A	B	C	D	E
60	45	30	20	10

(The exercises are the same and the time is measured in seconds.)

Obviously E is geared towards producing speed of movement, while D, C, B and A lean more and more towards speed endurance. The coach must select the appropriate duration. However, if a mix of different types of speed is required, then a programme such as the following may be used:

Alternative One

3 × E with a 30-second rest between sets. Complete each exercise before going on to the next, that is, 10 sec/rest, 10 sec/rest, 10 sec/rest. Then move on to the next exercise.

Alternative Two

1 × A with no recovery between exercises.

Alternative Three

1 × E, 1 × C and finally, 1 × A.

This is recommended only for advanced students!

This method can be applied to most forms of training. For example, working at circuit training in the gymnasium can be adapted so students complete the maximum number of repetitions in a given time. Bear in mind that duration of the work period will be specific to the type of speed required. The Polish have even developed a system of weight training ('speed weights') in which the student repeats an exercise as many times as possible in a set time. Alternatively, the student is timed with a stopwatch to see how long it takes to complete a given number of repetitions. The time unit and the number of repetitions must be carefully selected to achieve the precise training effect.

Safety is a very important factor to consider when moving any weight or load at speed. Before undertaking speed training, it is essential that the individual is well conditioned, is technically competent, and is either supervised, or has the knowledge to follow safe training practice. If in doubt, seek expert advice or failing that, choose another activity which will achieve the same ends.

Speed Training – Some Further Considerations

Speed training is anaerobic insofar as it demands maximum effort over short periods of time. Training at lower intensities will not improve speed, so the issue of rest must be carefully considered from the start. Speed training also requires a great amount of neuromuscular co-ordination. When this is fatigued, speed is impaired, so it is essential that all speed training is carried out with a rested system. Normally this would mean speed training at the start of the session, but by giving enough rest, it can be included later. The 100% effort required restricts work periods to 60 seconds or less, followed by a rest phase of at least three times the work period. The rest period is even longer when training for absolute maximum speed.

The coach must have some means of assessing work rate, such as counting the maximum number of repetitions performed in a set time, or measuring the heart rate during periods of maximum activity. A stopwatch is very useful for speed training.

The following are two examples of limb speed training drills:

1. Select a period of time – say 15 seconds.
   Then select a technique and count the maximum number of repetitions which can be performed in that time.
   Allow a rest period of 45–60 seconds.
   Then repeat the exercise, but this time try to beat the original number of repetitions.
   Perform up to ten sets, with appropriate rests.
   Over a period of time, the number of repetitions in each unit of time will increase.

This drill allows large groups to work at their own speed, but it does have a drawback, insofar as improvement comes only when whole techniques are added to the previous best; fractions of technique do not count! This difficulty can be overcome with the second drill.

2. Select a technique.
   Then time how long it takes a student to perform 5, 10, or 15 repetitions.
   This method permits monitoring of improvement reflected in fractions as small as 1/100ths of a second.
   The rest periods and number of repetitions are the same as for the first drill.

It is ESSENTIAL that increases in speed are not brought about through undesirable modification of technique.

Work periods of up to 60 seconds' duration develop speed endurance and this allows the student to train at high intensity even though fatigue is being experienced. Obviously the longer the periods of work, the longer should be the recovery. It would not be unreasonable to allow rests of up to six times the work period, and where absolute performance is required, even longer rests may be in order. Work may be resumed when the heart rate has returned to within 10–15 beats of normal.

The number of repetitions in each set will vary from individual to individual, so as a rule of thumb, allow the activity to last until technique just begins to suffer. It is better still to err on the side of caution and stop before this happens, not just for the sake of technique, but in the interests of personal safety as well. Speed training stresses the body to its limits, so there is always a risk of injury.

Methods to assist the development of pure speed can be used. These use pulleys, ropes, rubber bungees and springs to assist the limb to move at speeds greater than normally possible. However, it is worth stressing that limbs moving at speed are at risk.

It is difficult to isolate speed and/or strength when power is required. The essential thing to remember is that when training for power, loads must be light enough to allow maximum possible speed of movement. Use pulleys, springs, ropes and rubber bungees, plus anything else that will achieve the same effect.

Fig. 80 Using a rope the coach can pull the limb through faster than the student could on his/her own

Fig. 81

Flexibility

Most coaches and students of martial art would agree that flexibility and/or mobility are both essential prerequisites for good technique. Let's begin by clarifying just what is meant by 'flexibility'. We might say that 'flexibility is the range of possible movement in a single joint (such as the hip joint), or a series of joints (such as make up the spine)'. Do understand that flexibility is specific to a joint. The human body contains many joints, some of which may be unusually flexible, some flexible, and some no more than average. It therefore follows that one cannot really speak of a 'flexible individual'.

Bear the following points in mind when speaking of flexibility:

- some joints have a bony structure which limits the range of possible movement (e.g. knee, elbow);
- flexion of joints may be limited by intervening muscle in the case of heavily muscled individuals.

These are both mechanical limitations to movement and they cannot be significantly modified. Notwithstanding the above examples, limitation of the range of movement is generally imposed by those soft tissues which surround the joint. These are:

- muscle and fascial sheath;
- connective tissue (tendons, ligaments & joint capsules);
- skin.

Our main interest is in these three tissues because it is there that training can have a significant effect in terms of improving the range of movement and joint performance.

When muscle is stretched, the more it elongates and the greater the stretching force that is required. The muscle's resistance to stretching does not lie in the contractile mechanisms of the muscle itself, but in the fascial sheath that covers the muscle and the individual fibres which make it up. If we consider the factors which cause resistance to movement in a joint, we note the following approximate breakdown:

Skin	12%
Muscle	42%
Tendon	11%
Joint capsule	35%

The range of movement which can be attained at a joint can be broadly defined as:

Static flexibility The range of movement that can be maintained in a joint in a 'held' position.

Dynamic flexibility The range of movement that is attained momentarily in a joint during the course of an action or technique.

An individual might well have good static flexibility, yet his techniques may not require that range of movement at a joint. Conversely, an individual might lack sufficient static flexibility, yet be able to overcome this by the momentum of a limb which increases the range of movement during the performance of a technique. However, it is quite clear that dynamic flexibility is dependent on static flexibility.

Whichever type of flexibility is sought, you will need to consider what is called 'the stretch reflex'. The muscle and connective tissue surrounding most of the major joints are rich in nerve receptors which are sensitive to the degree of stretch in that tissue. They function as safety mechanisms by preventing dangerous over-stretching of connective tissue and/or joints. The nerve receptors cause the over-stretched muscles to contract and thereby prevent further elongation. Obviously this effectively reduces, or modifies, the range of movement. It therefore follows that slow stretch activities, where the joint and its associated tissues are slowly moved to their maximum range of movement and held there, are preferable to jerking or bobbing stretch-type activities which tend to more readily evoke the stretch reflex.

A further consideration is that a joint, or a series of joints, can be moved through their greatest range of movement by the effort of the individual concerned. This is known as 'active mobility'. Quite obviously the student is in full control at all times, so training becomes safer and the point at which the stretch reflex occurs can be carefully monitored. 'Passive mobility' training, on the other hand, occurs when a training partner, or equipment creates the movement. Though this can achieve a greater degree of movement, an over-enthusiastic or ill-informed action may cause injury.

Proprioceptive Neuromuscular Facilitation (alias 'PNF')

There has been a new development in mobility training during the last few years. This makes use of the body's own safety mechanisms to increase the range of movement in a joint. 'PNF', or to give it its full

Fig. 82 A good range of active mobility in the shoulder girdle

Fig. 83 Note the increase in range of movement when a partner helps in moving the hands closer together

name, 'Proprioceptive Neuromuscular Facilitation', stretches a muscle during its relaxation phase, immediately after it has been contracted. To make use of the concept, you must strongly contract those muscles which resist the range of movement in a joint. When the muscles relax afterwards, they lengthen more readily than usual and thereby increase the range of movement.

Use a partner to obtain maximum benefit from PNF training, though you can train on your own. Sit on the floor with both knees bent and the soles of your feet touching. Pull your feet close in to gain the best effect. Your partner carefully pushes both knees apart and down. Try to resist the pressure by forcing your knees up, maintaining this response for a count of five seconds. Then relax and let him push your knees down once more. You will find that your legs will open wider than they did previously.

I want to stress that great care must be taken when working on flexibility with a partner.

Fig. 84

Fig. 85

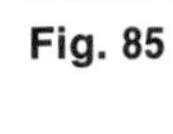

Fig. 86 Compare the effects of PNF exercises with active and passive mobility, fig. 81 and 82. Here the student is trying to pull both arms forwards against the gentle but firm resistance of a partner

Fig. 87 Any improvement?

Flexibility Training

It is said that improvements in technique will only come about through increases in mobility. Therefore the place of flexibility training in the overall programme is crucial. Interestingly, it is the least demanding in terms of physical work or specialist equipment. Nevertheless, there are sophisticated gadgets on the market which claim to dramatically improve mobility, but acceptable results can be obtained just as well without them.

I shall follow my system of dividing up the body into four main areas. Just to remind you again, these include:

- the arms and upper body,
- the trunk,
- the legs (including the hips),
- the whole body.

Develop a flexibility routine on the basis of circuit training, working each part of the body in turn. Try for as many circuits as appropriate, going around once as part of a warm-up, and perhaps twice or three times for a proper mobility session.

In the following examples of mobility training I will show how different techniques can be used for developing flexibility. Obviously it would be impossible to cover all exercises and needs but as I have said before, a little imagination will allow the coach to adapt some techniques and activities to meet his exact requirements.

Wrists and Shoulders

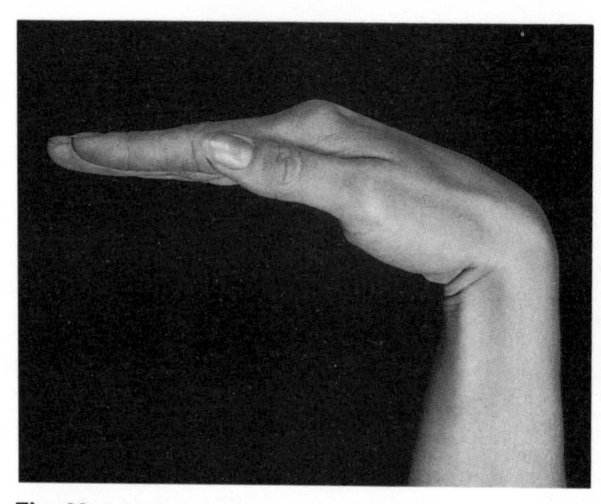

Fig. 88 A flexible wrist . . .

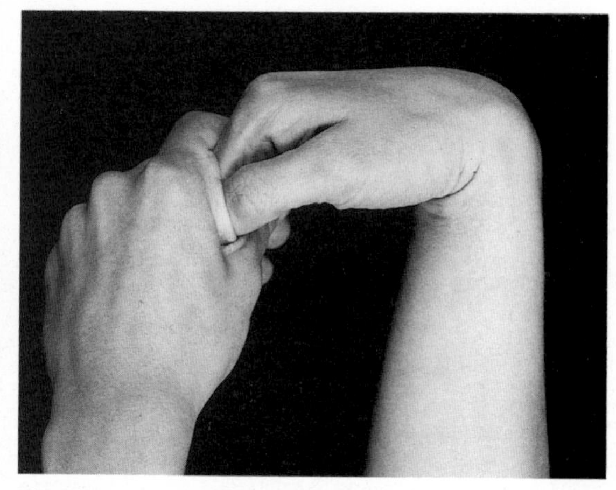

Fig. 89 . . . can be helped

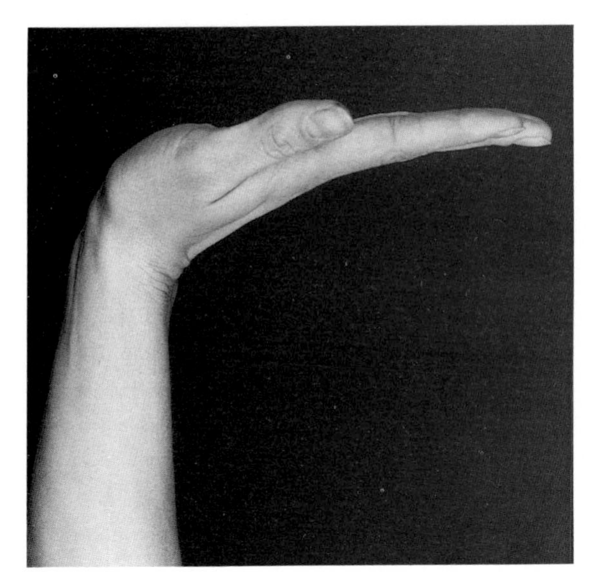

Fig. 90 With imagination . . .

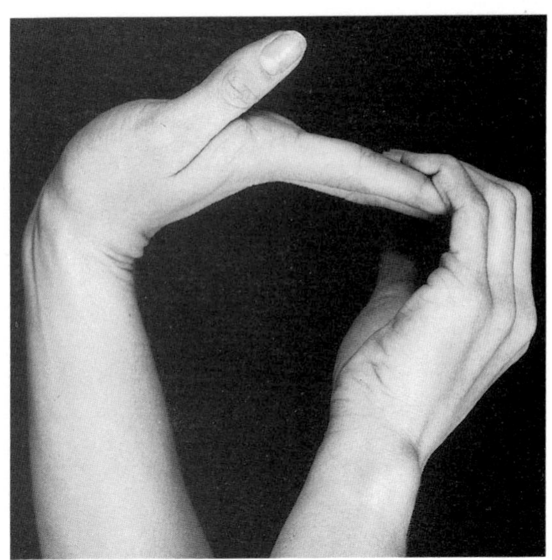

Fig. 91 . . . in any direction

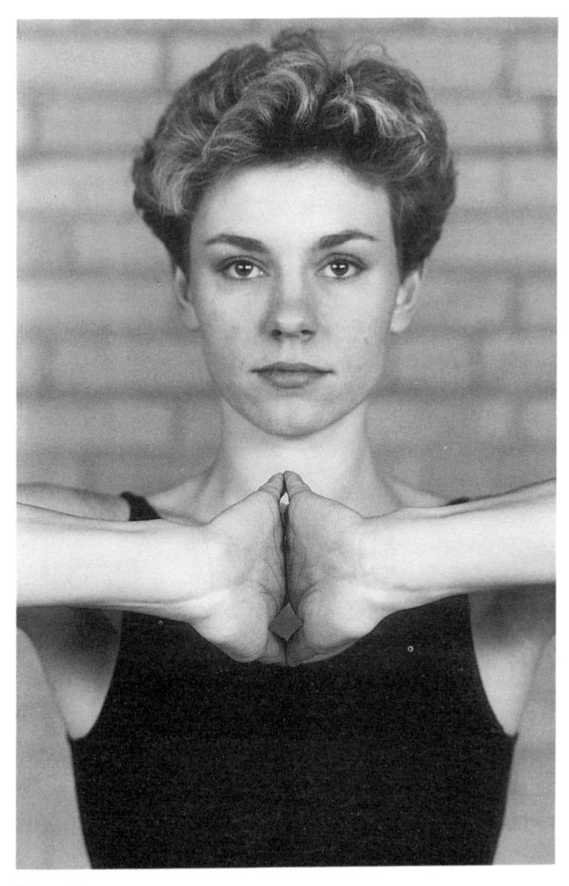

Fig. 92

Fig. 93 Arm circling. Rotating the arms backwards or forwards either together or individually develops excellent shoulder mobility

Fig. 94

Fig. 95

Fig. 96

Fig. 97 Link the fingers behind the back and lift them as high as possible

Fig. 98 If it is not possible to link the fingers a rope can be put to good use

Fig. 99 A variation on a theme. The fingers can be linked the other way too!

Fig. 100 Once again rope can be used to help

The Trunk

Fig. 101 Lower back mobility can change this . . .

Fig. 102 . . . to this

Fig. 103 By gently lifting the shoulders it can be improved

Fig. 104 For advanced students a partner can help

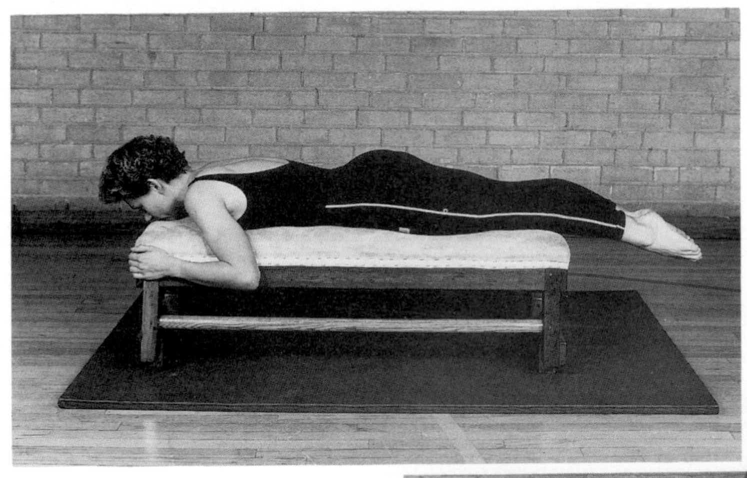

Fig. 105 Equipment such as a bench . . .

Fig. 106 . . . can be very useful

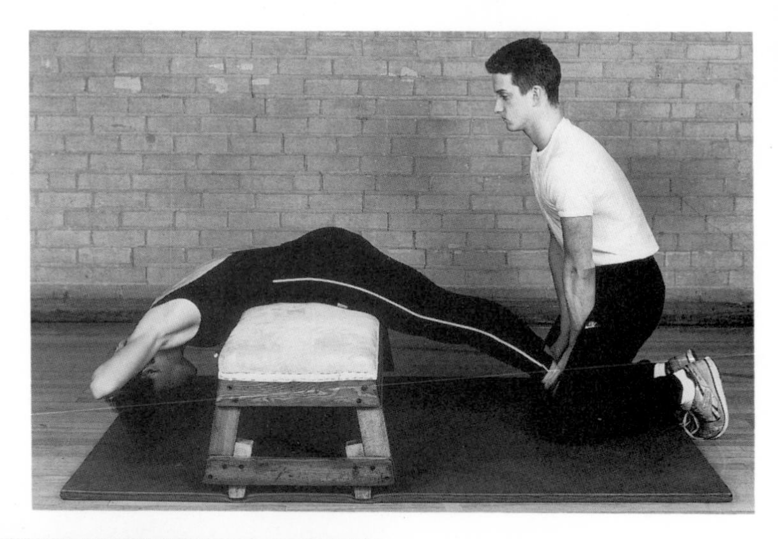

Fig. 107 For the advanced student using both equipment and a partner there are even more possibilities

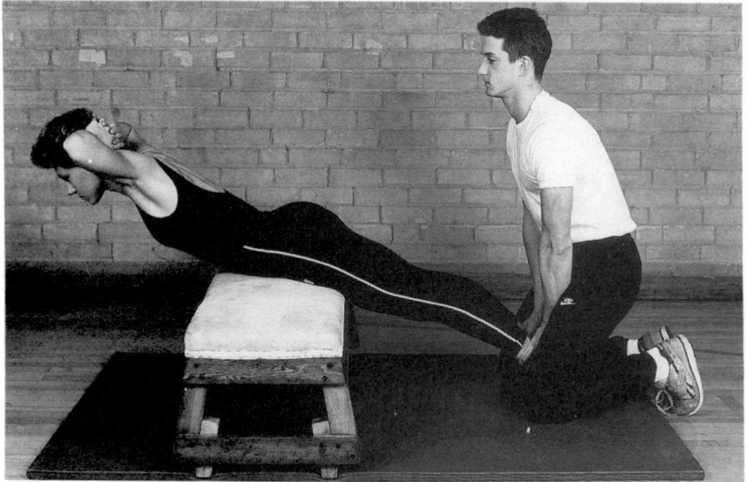

Fig. 108

Fig. 109

Fig. 110 Side lifts can be useful both to the right and the left

Fig. 111 Standing trunk twisters using a cane to keep the shoulders back. This exercise can be performed with the other foot forward as well

Fig. 112

Fig. 113 Bent over trunk twisters

Fig. 114 Turning to the left . . .

Fig. 115 . . . then to the right

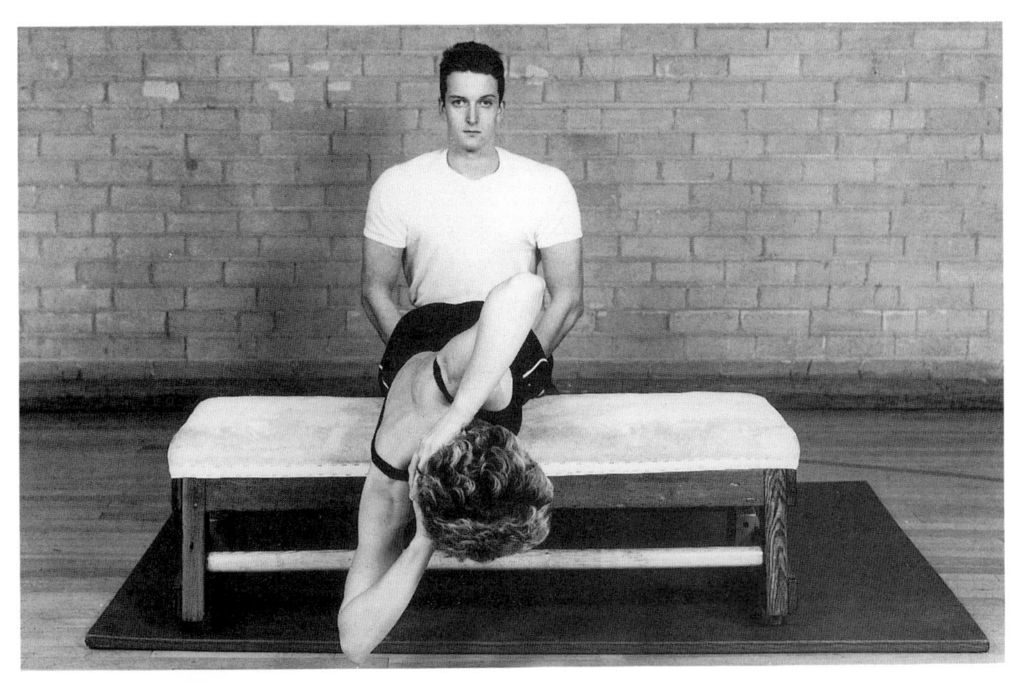

Fig. 116 For the advanced student the effect can be improved using simple equipment

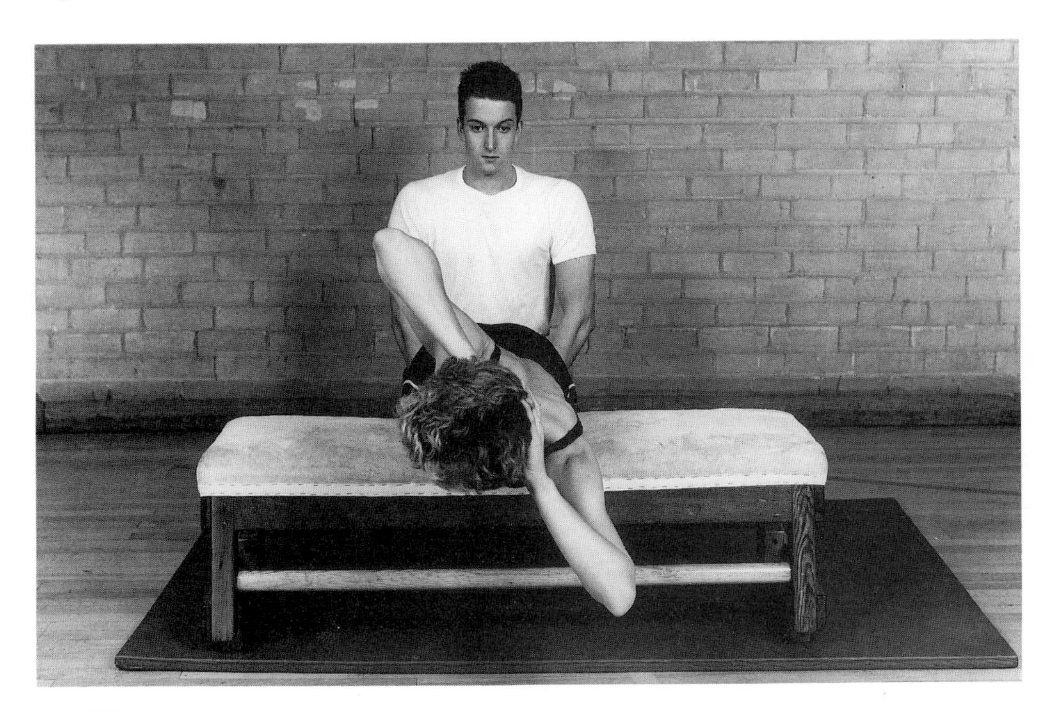

Fig. 117

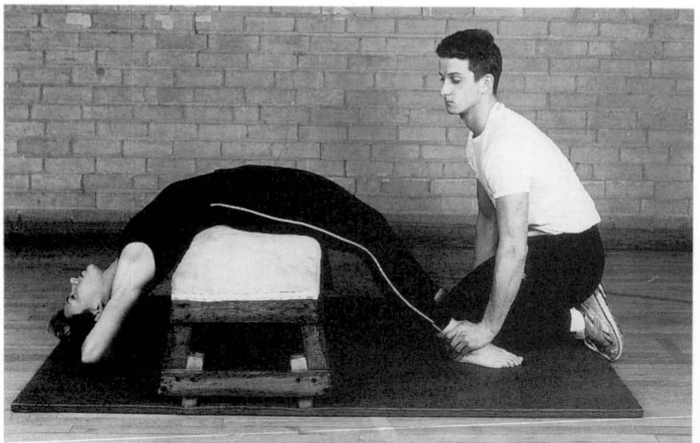

Fig. 118 For the advanced student mobility in a slightly diffferent plane might be useful

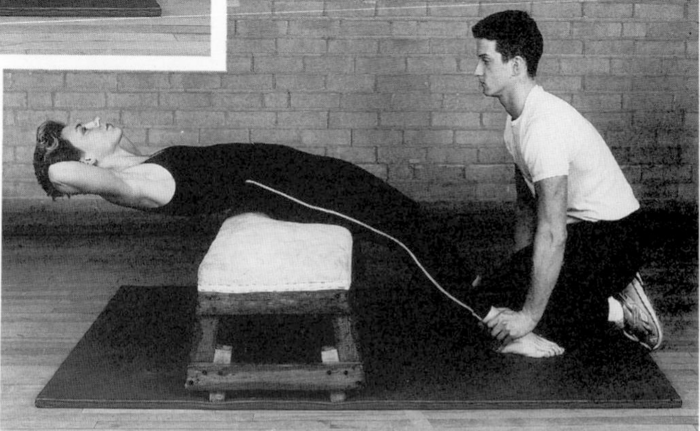

Fig. 119

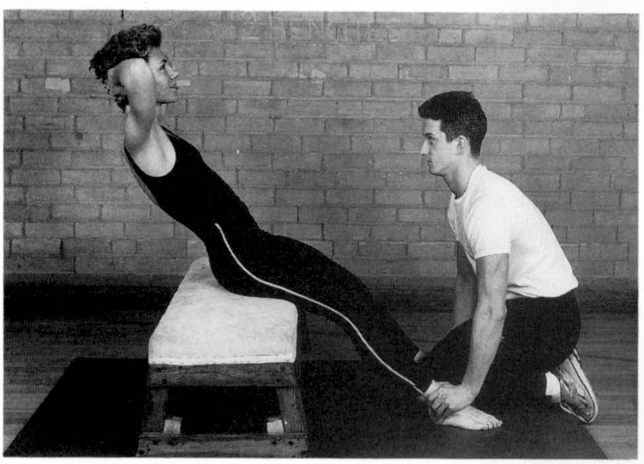

Fig. 120

Fig. 121

The Legs and Hips

Fig. 122 Calf stretches. Alternatively push the heels of the feet to the floor

Fig. 123 Hamstring stretches. From a poor press-up position keeping legs straight and palms of hands flat on the floor . . .

Fig. 124 . . . walk on tip toes to bring the feet . . .

Fig. 125 . . . as close to the hands as possible!

Fig. 126 The treadmill. Starting with the knee between the hands try to create as wide a split as possible between the thighs

Fig. 127 Change over the position of legs

Fig. 128 The hips can be worked in different ways. Feet as far apart as possible

Fig. 129 Reach as far forward as possible

Fig. 130 The classic hurdle sit position. Performed with the right or left foot forward

Fig. 131 A variation with the head being pushed down to the knee

Fig. 132 For the advanced student a further variation!

Fig. 133 Wall bars and a partner can add a useful extra dimension to standard exercises

Fig. 134

Fig. 135

Fig. 136

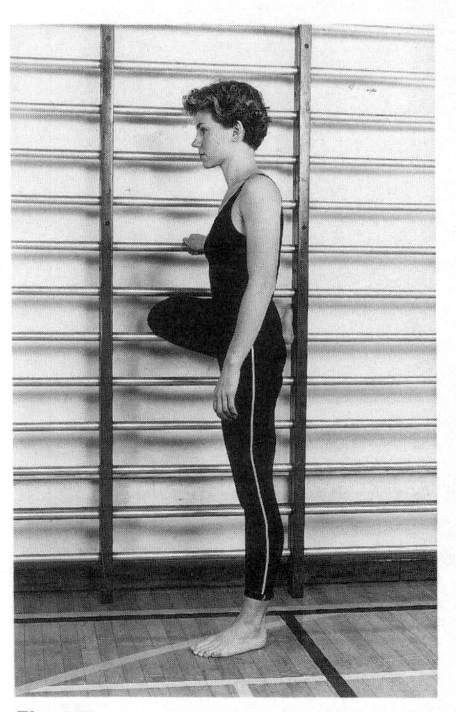

Fig. 137

Fig. 138

The Whole Body

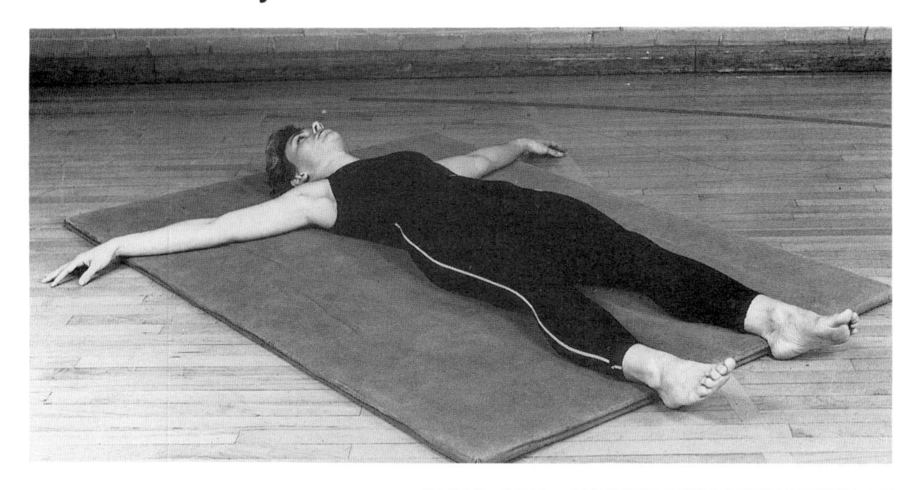

Fig. 139 The crucifix

Fig. 140 Right, foot to left hand!

Fig. 141 Left foot to right hand!

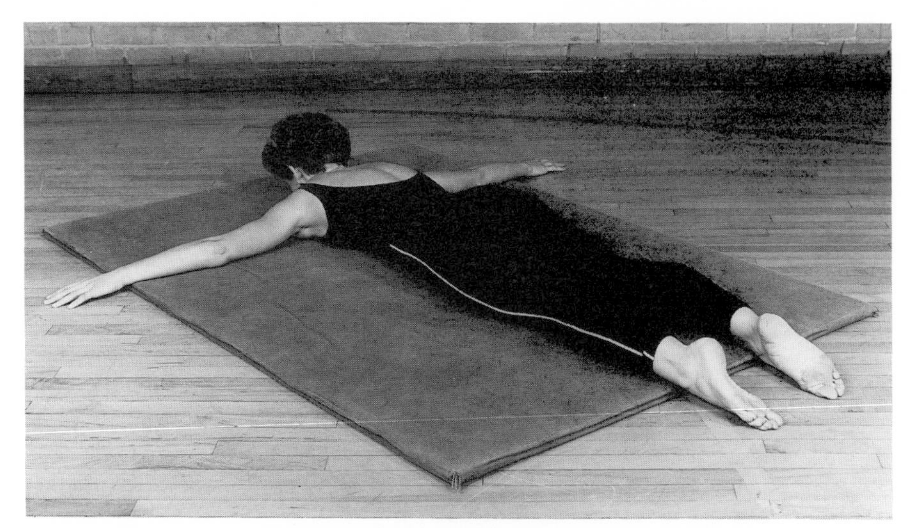

Fig. 142 The reverse crucifix

Fig. 143 Right foot to left hand!

Fig. 144 Left foot to right hand!

Endurance

Endurance is a vital component of martial art performance. Students must have the general endurance to be able to train for up to two hours, during which they generate very intensive but short-duration work rates. Competitive martial artists require the ability to sustain long periods of training, and then to work for a short period at an extremely high work rate. We must therefore consider two types of endurance. These are:

The aerobic system This provides a long-duration but essentially low level of energy output, which is generated when sufficient oxygen can be transported to active muscle and associated tissues to meet the demands of the activity. The presence of sufficient oxygen allows efficient utilisation of energy stores in the tissue without producing obstructive waste products, such as lactic acid. Fatigue is caused by the build-up of these wastes, rather than through depletion of energy stores.

The anaerobic system This provides a short-duration, high level of energy output which outstrips oxygen uptake by the active muscles. Lactic acid is produced as waste and as levels increase, the system slows down and eventually stops. A high rate and depth of breathing continue even after the strenuous exercise stops. This is to supply the oxygen needed to break down the accumulated waste lactic acid. The amount of oxygen actually required for this to occur is usually referred to as the 'oxygen debt'.

Don't get the erroneous idea that these two systems operate independently of each other. Though they are separate systems, they are mutually dependent, and it is essential to create a sound aerobic endurance upon which to develop a high level of anaerobic endurance. This is very much the case with younger students. The cardiovascular (the heart and blood vessels) and circulo-respiratory systems (the lungs and oxygen transport) must be trained to allow rapid transport of oxygen and nutrients to active tissue, while at the same time washing out carbon dioxide and other waste products. This will benefit both aerobic endurance, which requires the oxygen, and anaerobic endurance, which depends on removal of harmful waste products.

This interplay between the two systems can be said to provide four types of energy-producing pathways. These are:

Immediate – lasts up to 5 seconds,

Short-term – lasts up to 15 seconds,

Medium-term – lasts up to 45 seconds,

Long-term – lasts as long as is required.

Immediate, short- and medium-term systems are all anaerobic, and produce high levels of energy which diminish with time. The longer the activity continues, the greater becomes the contribution of the aerobic system.

Applying Endurance to Training

How does one design an endurance programme for the martial arts? What are the parameters to be considered? We know that the programme must help students to work at a variety of intensities, over different time units. Students must be fit enough to withstand the rigours of a training session lasting up to two hours. The programme must go further even than that. It must simultaneously achieve the best possible training effect whilst allowing the student to fully benefit from the coach's expert tuition. Only being able to participate for half of a lesson is unsatisfactory both from a learning, and from a financial point of view.

Different types of endurance may be required in any one lesson and the split for one school may be quite different from that required in another. Furthermore, the endurance needs of a male karate international in his early twenties will be completely different from those of, say, a middle-aged female who trains both to improve her self-confidence and her ability to protect herself. Yet some classes might include both extremes!

What, then, are the general points to be considered? Firstly, all martial artists need a fair standard of aerobic endurance capacity, if only to enable them to get the maximum benefit from an entire lesson. This may well prove adequate for those students who fall into the young, old, or recreational categories. Provided this endurance is on tap, then it is feasible to begin short periods of anaerobic, higher-intensity activity. For those students who have set their sights somewhat higher, these anaerobic intervals can be gradually increased in both load and duration, but in all cases the programme MUST be related to the needs of the individual student.

Ask most people to describe endurance exercises and they will immediately think of running and circuit training. Though both of these activities are effective, they need be neither the only, nor the main activity. In fact, the best form of endurance training for martial art uses the activity itself. The coach simply selects those skills and activities which can be adapted to produce the required training effect. The programme which he then designs is based upon the following three elements:

- Intensity – as a percentage of maximum performance,
- Duration – how long the exercise lasts,
- Frequency – how many times an exercise is repeated.

Endurance Training

Though the theory behind different endurance training programmes comes from athletics, the principles can nevertheless be adapted for martial art usage. Athletics scores heavily in that it uses an easy measure of performance – time. For example, if an athlete can run a best of 400 metres in 50 seconds, then 75% of maximum effort works out at running the 400 metres in 62.5 seconds. Perfectly good training regimes can be devised from such simple assumptions, so how can the martial arts coach adapt this measurement principle?

1. Select a martial art technique and count how many repetitions the student can perform in, say, 30 seconds. Multiply this figure by 2 and it will give a theoretical maximum minute work rate at 100% effort.

2. This method uses the pulse as an indicator of work rate. Select martial art techniques and make the student work flat out for 30–60 seconds. Measure his pulse immediately after exercise ceases. Count for ten seconds and mutliply the result by six. A pulse of 180 is equivalent to working at 100% effort.

There are things which you should know before relying on pulse measurements to indicate work loadings. Firstly, be aware that from 25 years of age, the pulse declines naturally with age by approximately 10 beats for every 10 years. This is an effect of age, not fitness. Therefore take the student's age into consideration. Refer to the diagram to see how the pulse declines with age and further, how it responds to different training loads. Secondly, at any age the heart of a female beats faster by approximately eight beats per minute, than that of the equivalent male. Take this also into account when using the pulse to measure workload.

The zones on the diagram marked 1, 2, 3 and 4 indicate heart rate response to workload, where 1 is a moderate response, 2 is a hard response, 3 is difficult and 4 is an extreme response to a very heavy workload. Note how these zones are affected by age, and make the appropriate adjustments.

The coach can now begin to design endurance programmes, relying upon these admittedly crude, but nevertheless effective measures. The programmes will bring about improvement by varying the applied workload in terms of its intensity, duration and frequency, and I have listed some alternatives for you to consider.

Diagram 3 Heart Rate as an Indicator of Workload

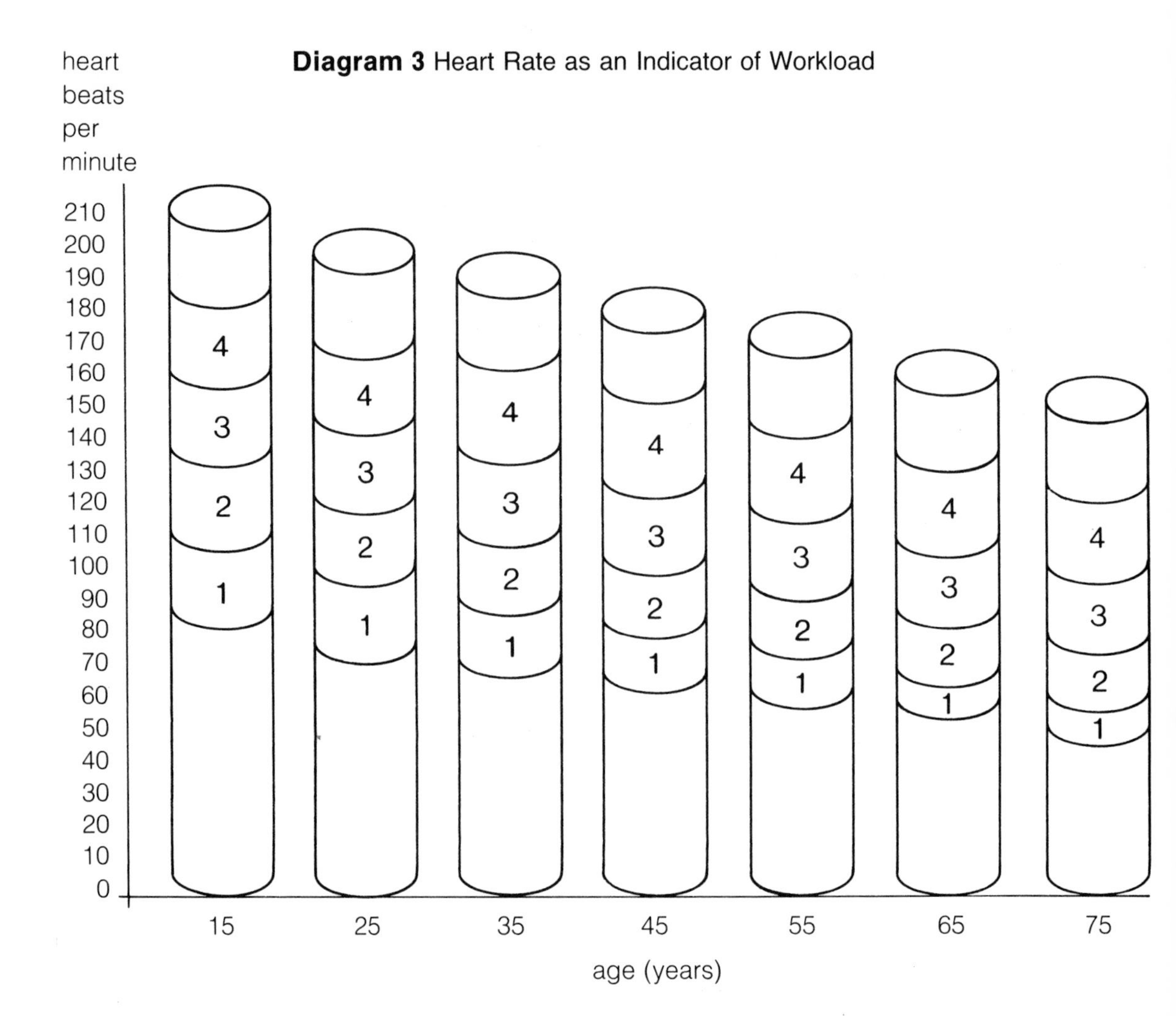

Continuous Work

This programme works the student at a loading which lifts the pulse into zone 1 on the diagram, a loading of 40–50% of the maximum work-rate. Aim to work for 10–15 minutes without a rest, extending this to 25–30 minutes in the case of more dedicated students.

Continuous Work – Sustained Effort

This programme increases loading so the pulse elevates into zone 2. This causes earlier onset of fatigue and hence a shorter exercise period. Aim to gradually build up to 5–10 minutes, with keener students progressing on to 15 minutes.

Repetition Training

This programme works students at competition/grading levels of intensity, over periods of 30–90 seconds (depending upon the needs of the individual). This elevates the pulse into zone 3 and represents a 100% workload. Allow an almost full recovery between bouts of work.

Fartlek (Speed Play)

This programme alternates intense with easy periods of activity and a typical scheme might work out something like this:

- 2 minutes' easy work at 40–45% loading. Pulse is not quite into zone 2,
- 1 minute's sustained effort at 60–65% loading. Pulse is not quite into zone 3,
- 1 minute's very easy work at only 30–40% loading. Pulse falls back toward resting levels,
- 30 seconds' maximum effort at 100% loading. Pulse not quite into zone 4,
- 2 minutes' easy work at 40–45% loading. Pulse not quite into zone 2,
- 45 seconds' maximum effort at 100% loading. Pulse rising into zone 4,
- 2 minutes' sustained effort at 60–65% loading. Pulse drops back into zones 3/4,
- 2 minutes' easy work at 40–45% loading and pulse not quite into region 2.

Interval Training

This is probably one of the most beneficial forms of endurance training and coincidentally, it is possibly the most misunderstood. Interval training was developed by a German sports physiologist named Gerschler and it is designed to develop the heart as a muscular pump in the same way that weight training develops other muscles. Gerschler discovered that the heart of the well-conditioned sportsman was most efficient when working at approximately 160 beats per minute. Higher or lower rates were found to be less efficient.

The principle of interval training is to select a workload that will raise the pulse to 160. More than that and the loading is too high, less and it is too low. Since the pulse indicates work-rate, it follows that many students can train together, each working at his individual intensity.

An interval training session might be arranged along the following lines:

- 30 seconds at 60% workload, so as to raise the pulse to 160,
- rest until the pulse drops to 120,
- repeat the 30-second work unit,
- repeat successive work/rest phases perhaps ten times in all.

Length of the recovery period is left to each individual and will depend upon that person's fitness. The pulse of fitter students falls back more quickly, so rest periods will be shorter. Students adjust their training load by returning to the three parameters we have already considered, viz., intensity of work, duration of the work unit and number of sets of work units.

Paarlauf (Pair Training)

This is a simple but elegant programme using training partners; one trains as the other rests! The workload is adjusted to allow an active period of around 30–45 seconds, and a recovery period while the partner works. Lighten the workload for less fit students, or put them into groups of three or four. The latter alternative extends the recovery period by the number of students working together.

I want to stress the importance of the rest period to endurance training. As your rule of thumb, allow rest of two to three times the duration of the work phase. So, a one-minute work phase will be followed by two or three minutes' rest. Adjust this according to the intensity of the work load, giving longer rests when necessary.

These various programmes have, as I said at the beginning of this section, been adapted from athletics. They are primarily aimed at developing aerobic endurance, though obviously by varying the duration/intensity/repetitions, they may also improve anaerobic capacity. The development of specific anaerobic endurance for the martial arts is more biased towards speed and strength endurance but this can be achieved by suitably modifying any of the programmes set out above.

(P)Sychology

It has long been held that good performance is made up of 1% inspiration and 99% perspiration! Whereas one might take issue with the exact proportions, most coaches and students would agree that any martial art discipline involves both a mental and a physical commitment. Unlike many sports, the martial arts have, it seems, long identified the correct mental approach needed to ensure optimum physical performance.

The degree of success which is achieved by the student/coach is based upon three broad areas of mental application.

Motivation

The martial artist who wishes to achieve the highest level of performance must have well developed self-motivation. Top performers are able to pull themselves out of the depths of despair when things are not going well, giving support to the saying 'when the going gets tough–the tough get going!'. In my opinion, this capacity to persevere through adversity separates the great martial artists from the amateurs and also-rans. Motivation cannot be trained in. It comes from two sources, which are:

- internal, arising out of the individual's all-consuming will to succeed,
- external, arising out of the help and encouragement provided by others (coach, family, friends, supporters, etc).

Determination

Determination might be described as long-term motivation, not just the desire to do well at a particular grading or event. Determination arises out of the modification of a student's lifestyle to ensure that energies are channelled into productive training, and that the martial artist operates within the philosophy and rules. Think of determination as the will to win.

Confidence

Top martial artists must have confidence in their own ability if they are to perform well. However, self-confidence must not cause them to underestimate an opponent's ability. They must be able to confidently adapt their performance to suit a situation, and when involved in a team event, must be confident in their ability to play a role.

The levels at which these three factors are maintained are also important. Performance will suffer equally if any one of the elements is under- or over-emphasized. To prevent either situation the coach must know his students, and how they react under stress. Once he has this knowledge, he can apply the correct form of arousal/calming and thereby ensure the best performance. Often this is overlooked by both student and coach, yet it is just as important as physical preparation. But how easy is it to monitor someone's state of mind, and to decide how far this should be altered? Knowledge of individual student behaviour is vital, and this can only come through a close association with that person. It is therefore not enough for the coach merely to train the student; at different times he must be prepared to act as teacher, friend, disciplinarian and confidant.

Skill

The single most important element in the practice of all the martial arts is the acquisition of skill, in the form of technique. The other components of fitness serve only to improve the physical and mental condition of students, so they can learn and apply those skills more easily. It is therefore essential that both coach and student be aware of the main aspects of skill acquisition. Let us begin by defining three broad areas:

1. Improvement in skill may come about simply as a result of the maturation process. Some of this improvement is not due to the

learning of skills at all. The adolescent student develops, in terms of skeletal and muscular co-ordination, and acquires an improved ability to self-monitor and correct. Thus we can see that what appears to be skill acquisition is actually deriving from improved faculties.

2. The purpose of training is to produce a technically effective response to a given stimulus. It is essential that the response conforms to correct performance criteria; an ineffective technique is one which does not so conform and the purpose of training is to eliminate it.

3. Skill is found in the performance of single acts or of a whole collection of actions. These may either take the form of a classical sequence, or of a rapidly changing response to a number of varying cues. However, any performance of skill can be affected by influences outside the student's immediate control. The performance of a kata, for example, can be very obviously affected by the training environment, the presence of onlookers, and the pressure of such things as gradings or competitions.

A modification of the neuromuscular system appears to accompany the learning of a skill. It is suggested that this modification may even extend so far as a change within the cerebral cortex of the brain itself. Make certain, then, that the correct skill is taught from the start, since it is virtually impossible to subsequently modify it! Training errors will have to be remedied as though training in a completely new skill.

The skill-learning process itself is far from straightforward. For example, new skills are not learned at a uniform rate. The introduction of new activities causes an immediate acquisition of skill. As training continues, the rate of acquisition begins to slow and eventually there is little or no further improvement. Skill acquisition is now said to be on a plateau. However, if training continues and a new incentive is provided, then a second bout of rapid skill-acquisition follows, though this is neither so rapid, nor for as long as the previous relevant period. A second plateau is reached and the cycle continues. A combination of good coaching and motivation will ensure that the student stays on the plateaux for the shortest periods and further, that he continues to work at attaining those fine aspects of technique which can be mastered only by spending a disproportionate amount of time on them.

The coach's ability to teach skills can be supplemented by a variety of means:

- by providing effective demonstrations,

- by using visual material such as video tapes of proficient exponents to ensure that the student knows exactly what is wanted of him,
- by providing effective feedback, so the student knows whether what he is doing is correct.

The coach must correctly identify the best method for introducing each new technique. Simple actions may be taught as a whole; more complex techniques may need to be broken down into a series of key units and when these have been learned, the series is re-integrated. Time allocation is important insofar as the student might be encouraged to work at a skill over many repetitions during a long period. Alternatively, the coach may suggest working at it in a series of short but intensive bursts, with periods of other activity in between. Whichever system you opt for, the fact remains that training in an enjoyable atmosphere helps in the learning and retention process.

A student's age can be critical in terms of the rate of skill-acquisition. I have already described how skill-acquisition is linked to physical growth in young students, but it is also markedly affected around the time of puberty (approximately 12–14 years for females and 14–16 years for males). It is interesting that ability to co-ordinate complex skills improves markedly after puberty. Therefore, skill acquisition for the young student should be geared to more general whole-body co-ordination activities, and intense specialisation of training should not take place until after puberty. It follows that girls can begin intensive skill acquisition earlier than boys, though societal pressures may influence the eventual prowess of some female students.

Time is one of the most difficult problems that a coach has to deal with, particularly since there are so many skills to learn, refine and modify. How often should a skill be practised to maintain form? Experiments in America have suggested that a complete two-year break was sufficient to reduce performance levels of the most complex skills to 60% of original levels. It follows therefore, that continuous practice is not needed, even were time available. Having said that, a certain amount of time must be set aside to maintain levels of performance. You can do no harm by 'over'-learning skills! These are retained better than skills which are merely experienced. A small amount of forgetting will be inevitable whatever the regime, but this should not be seen as a major difficulty.

Specific skill development can only be achieved by practising that specific skill. Practising other skills or components of fitness may well contribute, but not to a marked degree. Specific training applies that skill in highly specific situations, whereas general training simply provides more options for overall technical development.

The Martial Arts from a Fitness Point of View

As I have already said, the fitness requirements for martial arts differ greatly from one another and there is likely to be a marked difference of emphasis even within a particular discipline. Given this, I thought it might be helpful to look very generally at the martial arts, to see what elements of fitness are relevant.

Aikido

Aikido lessons generally last between ninety minutes and two hours. During this time, pairs of students perform skill work at a fairly constant speed. There is therefore a need for an aerobic fitness platform to act as the base upon which to build the specific requirements. Classical Aikido practice involves relatively little in the way of anaerobic work, though sport Aikido does exact an intensive workload during a timed two- or three-minute bout. This discipline requires the Aikidoka to work anaerobically for virtually the whole time in the two-against-one matches.

Classical Aikido involves little explosive action, while sport Aikido does – though not to the same extent as in some of the impact-based martial arts. Whole-body speed is of greater importance than limb speed, and agility is a high priority. Sometimes the Aikidoka performs a complex series of actions whilst moving in concert with the opponent. This requires a very high level of skill, often surpassing that found in the impact-based systems. Bear in mind that skill is best acquired during work that lies well within the aerobic band, when the neuromuscular system is unstressed.

Although Aikido eschews strength in favour of skill, it is clear that powerful movements pose no disadvantage. There may well be a case for a little light strength training in the arms and shoulders, though this can probably best be achieved through bodyweight exercises.

Aikido does not require a great degree of suppleness. There are no high kicks or contorted body positions, so that suppleness which is required will probably come about through training itself. The wrist joint receives a lot of pulling and twisting, so high-grade practitioners often seem to have a wider range of movement there than other martial artists.

Aikido emphasizes the psychological approach and rather than offer advice on how to improve this, I would like to recommend the Aikido method to other sports!

Full Contact

Full Contact is an extremely strenuous discipline, and like Aikido it is practised over periods of between 90 minutes and two hours. During this time, students train alone on basic techniques, or they work out with a partner. Training aids such as punching bags and target mitts are essential. Lower-level training requires good aerobic endurance, with an increasingly anaerobic emphasis as training nears a competition or grading examination. The aerobic base is best provided by standard methods, supplemented by light shadow-boxing and bag-work. Anaerobic work can be based upon any of the systems which I have already discussed, and in particular, I recommend high intensity bag-work against the clock. Since competition is held over three or more two-minute rounds, your training must use that cycle, with active rests between work periods.

Full Contact uses a lot of explosive action originating from the legs and arms. Plyometric training could be useful here! Squat- and skip-kicking exercises are particularly useful, teaching how to move explosively from a moving stance. Whole-body and limb speed are of equal importance, and when a limit is reached, I recommend strength work such as explosive press-ups and half squats. Weight training is helpful, though you should concentrate on shifting light weights at high speeds. However, beware of unwelcome technique modifications when you do this!

The skill element in impact systems is lower than that required in the grappling disciplines but it is still best learned when the neuromuscular system is rested. Practise the technique form by working at a low intensity against the bag. Then improve impact with higher-speed work that lifts you above the anaerobic threshold.

Full Contact techniques involve high kicks in which hip abduction and extension are limiting factors. Begin with PNF stretching routines and when the required degree has been achieved, you can switch over to dynamic mobility work against the bag.

Full Contact training is arduous, so motivation is an essential ingredient for success. You have to clearly defeat the opponent, so generate aggression within the rules.

Hapkido

I hope that Hapkido performers will not be offended if I describe their discipline as a sort of halfway house between Aikido and Karate. Hapkido involves not only the punches and high kicks of the striking disciplines but it also includes a large repertoire of grappling and throwing techniques. The fitness requirements therefore span the whole range of activity. Regardless of what precise form practice takes, I advocate developing enough aerobic endurance to last through the typical lesson. Like most martial arts, this lasts for between an hour and two hours. If nothing else, a level of aerobic fitness will allow many technique repetitions, whether in class lines, or in pair-form activity.

Lower grades need comparatively little anaerobic endurance, though this requirement increases as the grading examinations become more complex. Even so, we are speaking of intense work for periods of no more than two minutes' duration. Usually this is concentrated in the impact side of the syllabus, so I would recommend timed, intense work against the bag and the target mitts.

The grappling techniques require agility and a high level of skill, for they are applied on the move. Impact techniques benefit from explosive action and some plyometric training would yield benefits. Once again, both whole-body and limb speed are of equal importance: switch over to strength training when you reach your speed limit. The skill element should be learned during the early parts of the lesson, or by working two different parts of the body consecutively. Hapkido's high kicks need good flexibility in the hip, so stretch the hip adductors and flexors using the PNF method, then begin dynamic mobility work against a bag.

Like Aikido, Hapkido makes much of the correct mental approach and I do not feel able to improve upon the drills suggested in the traditional schools.

Jiu Jitsu

Jiu Jitsu is the forerunner of Olympic Judo, but unlike the latter, it has retained a number of striking techniques. Having said that, these are neither so developed, nor so diverse as those found in Hapkido. Typically they are low-impact strikes designed to cause a diversion, during which time a grappling technique is applied. Jiu Jitsu lessons last for between one and two hours and typically proceed at a regular rate which is well into the aerobic band. More technique repetitions will become possible if the Jiu Jitsuka takes up any of the general aerobic training regimes.

Practice is usually in pairs, with each partner taking turns to apply a technique. The resting partner has time to recover before taking over the active role once more. Sometimes one student takes on a series of consecutive attacks, and energy needs then tip into the anaerobic band, though they are never as intense as in activities such as Full Contact. Having said that, the gradings become gradually longer and more involved, so the anaerobic requirement does increase with advancement in grade. A certain amount of explosive action is used when the techniques are properly delivered, so plyometric leg exercises would probably help in this respect. Jiu Jitsu uses mainly whole-body speed as opposed to limb speed, and exercise drills such as harness-sprints might yield a useful benefit. Jiu Jitsuka move bodymasses at speed, so I recommend weight training using nothing more than 70% loadings, moved as quickly as possible during a short work-period.

Jiu Jitsu techniques are often long and involved, requiring a very high level of skill, agility and coordination. They are also varied, so a different skill can be taught over several successive techniques without tiring the neuromuscular systsem. There is no need for any specific flexibility work; that which is required will come naturally through training itself.

Jiu Jitsu is not a gentle art and the practitioner must expect practice to be robust. Therefore concentrate on developing your mental approach to the activity.

Karate

Karate is an impact-based activity though it is not nearly as strenuous as Full Contact. Having said that, one form of Karate does engage in Full Contact-like activities, so the same comments apply to both disciplines. Karate lessons last between 90 minutes and two hours, with students training on basic techniques in class lines, or practising several types of sparring with a partner. Training aids are not common, though one school uses the impact pad to develop striking force. Training requires a high level of aerobic endurance, with an increasingly anaerobic bias as training nears a competition or grading examination. The aerobic base comes from general training, supplemented by light running, swimming, or speed weights.

Anaerobic work is most effectively performed using Karate kata. Some of these are quite long sequences of movements. They also teach conditioned reflex associations, combining blocks with counter-attacks, etc., so they are very useful indeed. Karate bouts last two or three minutes so build your training drills on that requirement, breaking each work period with active rest intervals.

Karate relies heavily upon explosive action in both legs and arms. Plyometric training is therefore essential. Analyse your kicking and punching actions and design drills to pre-stretch the muscles used. Squat- and skip-kicking exercises work well for the legs, explosive press-ups and certain medicine ball drills work the arms. Whole-body and limb speed are equally important, so devise relevant drills using harness-runs and bungee elastic attached to the wrist and ankles. Beware unwelcome technique modifications! Weight train by pumping light weights at high speeds over short time periods.

Pack skill-acquisition into Karate training by alternating arm and leg activities. Work on the hips to develop sufficient flexibility to be able to kick to the head with a variety of techniques. Increase your hip abduction, extension and circumduction. The first two are best improved by PNF methods, the latter by slow dynamic mobility drills performed afterwards, when the body is loosened up.

Classic Karate practice teaches the appropriate psychology. The psychology of modern sport Karate, however, has much in common with other competitive disciplines.

Kendo

Kendo is an impact-based activity using a bamboo sword known as a **shinai** and a full set of head and upper-body armour. Kendo lessons last between 90 minutes and two hours, with students exercising, or training with a partner. Training requires a high level of aerobic endurance, because of the vigorous sparring that lasts for three-quarters of the entire training session. Not all of this is flat-out, however; there is a great deal of to-ing and fro-ing interspersed with peaks of intense and explosive activity.

The aerobic base could be improved by any of the typical training regimes, and perhaps the whole-body involvement of swimming would prove most useful of all. Anaerobic work could adapt the basic practice known as **suburi**, or 'cutting the air'. This would provide a tailor-made regime if performed full-force and against the clock. Competition bouts last two minutes, so high-level preparation work should be based upon this time period. Kendo relies heavily upon explosive action in the arms, so it follows that plyometric training will be of benefit. I would advise incorporating the bamboo shinai into any drills that you devise.

I hope Kendoka will forgive me when I say that the degree of skill needed to deliver a cut to **men** is less complex than that required by, say, an Aikidoka applying the technique known as **nikkyo**. In saying this, I am not denigrating the skill needed to set up the cut, nor to create the opportunity for using it; I am referring merely to the mechanics of the cut itself. Much of the skill element required for Kendo can be acquired by training at a level of aerobic energy expenditure with a co-operative partner.

Flexibility in the shoulders is of major importance to Kendo practice. Passive and active stretching of the shoulder joints should be combined with suburi work, otherwise the muscles will contract and the range of movement will suffer.

Kendo practice is based upon an aggressive psychology, though the rules of competition contain the exuberance that is sometimes all too evident in free sparring, if the late and respected R.A. Lidstone is to be believed (and I'm sure he is!).

Kung fu

I never know quite how to deal with the Chinese martial arts. There are so many of them, and all so different that it is virtually impossible to apply any meaningful series of general comments to them. I therefore propose to select three forms: a southern Shaolin form, a northern Shaolin form and an internal discipline. All three use individual practice during which the student proceeds at his own speed. The internal form uses less energy than either of the other two and all of its practice falls within the aerobic band. The two Shaolin forms are similar to Karate in their energy requirements, so it can be said that both require an aerobic base, supplemented with anaerobic training.

Kung fu lessons last between one and two hours, and training is either individual, or pair form. The internal system uses far less pair-form training than either of the others. The southern Shaolin system may use training aids such as the 'wooden man'. This is a target dummy used for practising strikes.

Anaerobic work can be effectively performed using long sequences of prearranged techniques which, in many ways, are similar to the kata of Karate. The internal system uses kata as the mainstay of its training, though the speed and power of movement are brought down well into the aerobic band. The southern Shaolin systems use a great deal of arm work, so local muscular endurance is needed to support various training regimes such as 'sticking hands'.

The internal form of Kung fu uses relaxed strikes and kicks. These are not energy-consuming and will benefit from no additional drills. Both of the Shaolin systems use a great deal of isometric activity, with muscles working hard against each other. This is facilitated by training drills which rely upon deep stances and spasm-muscle contraction. The southern systems sometimes use short-range strikes and this is much improved by training drills which use medicine balls thrown with nearly straight elbows. The northern Shaolin system will benefit from explosive leg work using plyometric principles.

The Shaolin systems sometimes use additional training drills designed to toughen the forearms, fingers and fists. From what I have seen of them, they appear to work quite effectively. Skill-acquisition work is done by training at lower speeds in both of the Shaolin systems. The internal form is able to concentrate on skill throughout the lesson because of its low energy requirement. The southern Shaolin system requires no additional flexibilty training but the northern system will benefit from attention to the hips.

The internal system contains its own in-built psychology. The other two use the pragmatic, 'if it works – use it' approach, where fighting efficiency is the only criterion for consideration. Some Shaolin systems have extremely sophisticated methods for suppressing fear and anxiety.

Shorinji Kempo

Shorinji Kempo is very similar in its content and fitness requirements to Hapkido. Having said that, it does differ with respect to its psychology. Shorinji Kempo regards itself as the vehicle for a particular form of Buddhist philosophy named **kongo zen**. This stresses reliance upon self and the cultivation of a clear and uncluttered mind.

Tang Soo Do

Tang Soo Do is similar to Karate in terms of its practice and fitness requirements. It does differ though in the increased usage of higher kicks, which require a great deal more flexibility work in the hips than either Karate or Full Contact. The action known as 'circumduction' plays a much larger part in the Tang Soo Do syllabus.

Taekwondo

Taekwondo is again very similar to Karate and Full Contact. Like Tang Soo Do, it stresses leg techniques more than the other two. Its energy requirements are closer to those of full contact because competition is multi-round and uses full-power blows and kicks. Taekwondo competitions use more kicks than any other martial art discipline, so a great deal of mobility/speed/leg endurance work is needed.

Thai Boxing

Thai Boxing and Full Contact have so much in common that fights between the two are often arranged. It therefore follows that fitness requirements are the same.

Food for Thought

The previous sections have attempted to look at the essential elements which have to be considered when devising training regimes. Strength, speed, suppleness, stamina, skill and elements of (p)sychology have been looked at in the very specific light of their application to the various martial arts. The last section looked specifically at the essential balance of these factors with respect to individual martial arts. It is this aspect to which the enthusiastic coach must now address his attention. How can he modify exercises or activities so that they are exactly what his students want? I thought it might be an idea to show how with a little imagination drills and practices can be designed to meet those requirements.

Most martial arts require flexible and strong wrists; the figures show a simple exercise to achieve both. However, others require highly specific movements demanding range of movement, speed and strength, particularly those involving weapons (see the figures 147–150).

Fig. 145 Disc weights can be used to develop strength in the wrists

Fig. 146

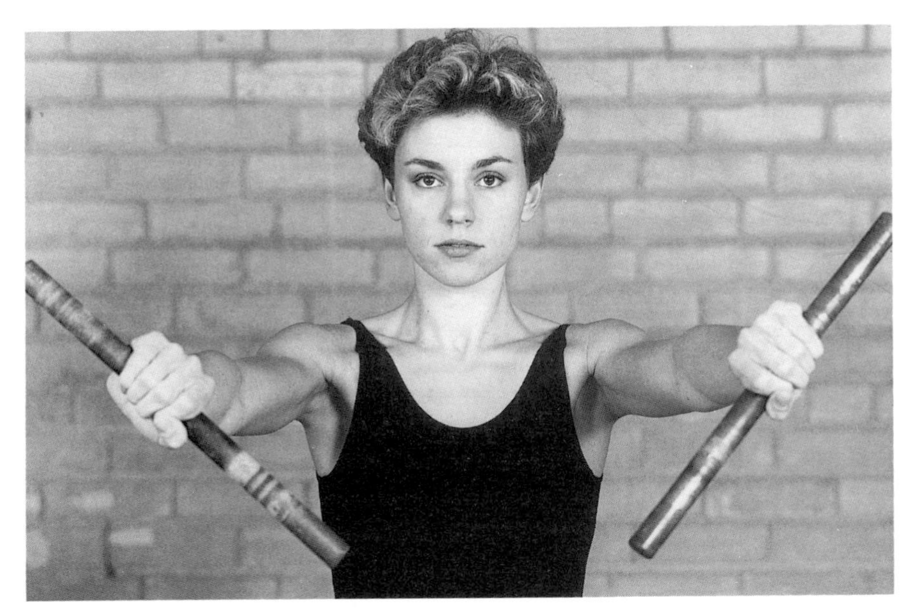

Fig. 147 Lifting bars can be used to develop hand, arm and shoulder strength in rotation

Fig. 148

Fig. 149 In flexion . . .

Fig. 150 . . . and rotation

With martial artists there seems to be a dilemma between strength and speed, especially when what really is needed is power! Even the simplest of exercises, the press-up, can be modified to suit the needs of everyone (see the Figures 151–158). In this example, by progressively removing the load from the shoulders the emphasis changes from strength to speed, or vice versa! Similarly many other activities can be modified to achieve the desired result.

Fig. 151 Using wall bars allows for the load to be varied in press-ups. As the student holds progressively higher, the load on the arms and shoulders becomes less. The exercise changes from a slow strength activity to a fast powerful action at speed

Fig. 152

Fig. 153

Fig. 154

Fig. 155

Fig. 156

Fig. 157

Fig. 158

Those martial arts which use punching techniques can also, with the aid of the simplest equipment – a skipping rope and a rubber quoit – develop not only strength and power, but the observant coach can also refine those essential elements of technique at the same time. Strength, speed, power and technique development can be achieved with not much more than a piece of string! In fact this idea can be used in a variety of ways. Those martial arts which require the use of weapons can use this technique in exactly the same manner. If the rope is attached to the weapon close to the handle section it can be used with a little imagination in the precise action of a specific technique. The figures 159 and 160 should give a few ideas.

Fig. 159 With a little imagination very specific strength training activities can be devised. Using a rope wrapped around a wall bar to create resistance by friction strength can be developed specifically. Punching

Fig. 160 The coach can increase the resistance by varying the pull on the rope or increasing the number of turns around the wall bar

For those martial arts which use kicking techniques, the figures 161, 162 and 163 should show how once again the simplest of equipment might be used to develop those very specific aspects required for excellence. Fig. 164 shows how bungee elastic can be used to develop, in this example, punching, but with a little ingenuity a whole variety of other techniques.

Fig. 161 Kicking

Fig. 162

Fig. 163 With variations

Fig. 164 Bungee elastic ropes can be used in a similar way

Even if wallbars are not available the coach should not be stuck. Perhaps freestanding practices as shown in the figures 165 and 166 might not only be an alternative but possibly more in keeping with the needs of the student and the technique. These few examples of a varied approach to the development of the essential elements of excellence of performance should give the coach and student an insight into how either techniques or drills can be adapted to develop those particular aspects which a student needs.

Fig. 165 Wall bars are not essential. The coach alone can create all the resistance

Fig. 166

Rehabilitation after Injury

A major problem facing injured martial artists is the attitude of many doctors toward what they see as self-inflicted injuries. However, as sporting activities continue to flourish, it is becoming increasingly possible to receive useful and constructive advice on rehabilitation following training injuries. The Martial Arts Commission operates a medical survey which regularly reports on the types and circumstances of the most common martial art injuries.

Fractures

Fractures are broken bones, caused by the direct or indirect application of force which exceeds the bone's tensile strength. A fracture may be no more than a hairline crack (a 'fissure fracture'), or it may be a shattered bone, perhaps with jagged ends poking through the skin. Any martial artist who considers that he may have a broken bone should consult the casualty unit of his local hospital. Not all fractures need plaster casts; sometimes a turn of tape is all the dressing required.

Whatever the type of fracture, it is essential to rest it so that the healing processes will not be disrupted. Rehabilitation begins immediately after treatment and consists of remaining as mobile as possible. A broken arm will not prevent leg workouts; neither will it prevent joint mobility work. A broken leg is far more difficult to deal with but ingenuity will nevertheless allow some form of training. Fractures to the spine or pelvis should be allowed to heal completely without any physical activity likely to place a strain on the mending surfaces. Therefore be prepared to forego your level of fitness until everything returns to normal.

Bruises

Without doubt, these are the most common martial art injuries. They are caused when an applied force damages the blood vessels, and allows blood to leak out into the surrounding tissues. Severe impacts on thinly-covered bones cause a rapid and substantial loss of blood that pushes up the tissues around it into a lump. This is called a haematoma and it is not an uncommon result of injury to the shin. Haematomas will eventually clear up by themselves, though this can take a long time. Alternatively, a surgical operation will drain the haematoma and allow you to train much earlier.

Bruises need no rehabilitation as such, except that of using the injured limb as soon as possible. If the bruise is very painful, and if it is likely to receive the odd knock, then you should wrap it well with a crepe bandage, and perhaps wear a shin guard or something similar over the top. If you have bruised your knuckles, then it would be as well to leave off aggravating the injury with further punching. Failure to let the injury heal will only prolong the time needed for a full recovery.

Hard kicks in the stomach area can cause serious internal bleeding and surgical shock. The martial artist feels dizzy and may pass out. If he then rallies, you should assume you are dealing with shock and take the victim to hospital as soon as possible. Sutured blood vessels must not be subject to stress, so rehabilitation consists of taking things easy until the repair is firm. Kicks to the kidneys can cause blood to appear in the urine. This is not often serious, though I would advise you to report the matter to your doctor. Rehabilitation consists of no more than allowing the kidneys to heal without further injury.

Hard blows to the chest can cause serious bruising and subsequent training must avoid further injury to the affected region. Female martial artists receiving a hard blow to the breasts should examine them for any odd lumps. If these are discovered, she should report the matter to her doctor. Prevention is better than cure and those who spar should buy proprietary breast protectors.

Nervous tissue can also be bruised and though the brain is well cushioned, it can be injured as a result of hard blows to the head. The impact shock waves pile delicate tissue against the skull and rip apart the tiny connections which carry nerve impulses. Severe impacts can also rupture the blood vessels in the head, causing bleeding into the brain tissue and very serious injury. At what stage does head injury become dangerous? A rule of thumb suggests that if the victim is dazed, or does not respond correctly to simple questioning, then you can assume that brain damage has occurred. Anyone who has been knocked senseless should be taken to a hospital casualty unit. Anyone who has been knocked out by a blow to the head, recovers and then passes out again requires emergency hospital attention.

Rehabilitation of head injury consists of allowing the tissues to heal. If this is done, other nerve cells take over the function of those destroyed and within six weeks or so, the martial artist is able to fully engage in training once more. This does not mean to say that he should not train during the interim, but if he does, then he should not take part in any activity where there is a likelihood of further head injury.

Joint injuries

Injured joints must be exercised as soon as possible after treatment has been received. The exception is where surgical intervention has taken place. In such a case, you must allow the stitches to heal before working the joint through its full range of movement, though there is nothing stopping you from training your other limbs. One of the main problems associated with joint injuries is muscle-wastage. This occurs at a rapid rate and is particularly noticeable following knee cartilage surgery. The best form of rehabilitation is to flex the muscles without producing joint movement, using the form of strength training referred to as isometric.

Where no surgery has taken place, rehabilitation should begin almost immediately. Train isometrically until the acute phase of the injury has passed, then gradually increase isotonic work and flexibility exercises. Joints are located by muscle tension, so it is important to ensure they are both strong and supple. If they aren't, then parts of the joint can move out of line and this can lead to rapid wear and inflammation. The knee joint is a case in point. Rehabilitate acute knee injury with low stances and non-jerky movements. Avoid twisting actions! Strengthen the muscles which help locate the knee joint by performing extension/flexion work against weights.

Again, prevention is better than cure and it may be possible to slightly amend your practice until it becomes less likely to cause injury. Do not train on mats which prevent your feet from pivoting freely, or which come apart. Do not kick or punch forcefully unless there is a resistance that stops movement before the joint is fully extended.

Shoulder joint injury occurs in the grappling-based martial arts, usually as a result of sudden leverage applied to the extended arm. The head of the humerus is forced through the joint capsule and much tissue damage occurs. Hospital attention is then needed to reduce the dislocation. Rehabilitation should begin immediately, and aim at maintaining mobility. A little later you should begin strengthening exercises, using various forms of press-ups, bench-presses and such-like. The shoulder will never be as strong as it was before and if it continues to dislocate, then surgical procedures may be necessary to reinforce the ruptured muscle.

Ankle injuries tend to occur more frequently when mats are used. Either the foot is prevented from turning freely, or individual mats come apart and trap the foot. The ankle turns inwards and ligaments are torn. As these heal, the split ends are joined by fibrous connective tissue which tends also to grow into neighbouring ligaments. The ankle then loses mobility and when weight comes down awkwardly upon it, the muscles relax to prevent injury and the ankle again turns under you. It is therefore important to properly rehabilitate a sprained ankle. Apply ice until the swelling is reduced and try to do without a supportive bandage if you possibly can. Work the joint through its full range of movement and massage it, using firm pressure to manipulate the tissues. A wobble board is one of the best rehabilitation aids for injured ankles. This is a flat, wide board atop a wooden hemisphere. Stand on the board and try to keep your balance and when you can manage, have a training partner throw you a medicine ball. Catch and return it without slipping off the board.

Lacerations

Lacerations vary from a burst blister to a great gash that needs stitches to draw the gaping wound edges together. Fortunately the latter is rarely encountered in martial art practice. The skin is very effective at preventing harmful bacteria from entering the body but when it is damaged, that protection is lost. You must therefore decide whether it is best to leave the wound, or to dress it with a protective covering. There is no doubt that exposed wounds heal more quickly when they aren't ground into the dirt, or have training tunics rubbed against them. If this is the case, then you should clean the skin around the wound with a mild, cleansing antiseptic solution, and then apply a waterproof dressing which you subsequently change frequently.

Cut or blistered feet should be dressed, and permission sought from the coach to wear training shoes until the injury has healed. Rehabilitation consists simply of allowing the skin to repair without subjecting it to further injury.

Writing the Programme

Before attempting to design the best training regime for any healthy individual, several key questions should be asked. The main considerations which I take particular cognizance of are as follows:

- Age
- Sex
- Height
- Weight (now, and that required for the sport)
- Present level of fitness (how is it to be assessed?)
- The required level of fitness (depends on ultimate goal)
- Specific fitness for a martial art (how is it to be assessed?)
- Competitive season (for those who compete)
- Grading timetable (for all students)
- Facilities available
- Time available per week to train
- Time of day available to train
- Level of commitment
- Level of aspiration

Coaches may well be able to identify other aspects of particular relevance to them, but I have found that these provide a reasonable basis for training schedule design. However, the answers do not tell you how to integrate a class, the members of which have different work-rates, aspirations and fitness!

It may be that height confers an advantage in a particular discipline. Is there an ideal weight, and do you know it? The amount of time which a student is willing to devote to training will obviously affect his rate of progress and ultimately, the level of performance achieved. As a matter of fact, even the time in the day when he trains may affect progress. Most students come directly to training after a hard day at work, and this is not conducive to achieving excellence!

The facilities too are critical, and taking an extreme example, a student will not be able to train at all if there is no club near to where he lives! The provision of essential equipment, or the lack of it, will affect the rate of learning and possibly even the final standard of performance achieved.

The most important question of all, perhaps, is what does the individual student want from his martial art? Some want to develop their confidence, others to defend themselves; not a few want to compete. This, coupled with a commitment to achieve that goal will ultimately affect how much work they are prepared to take on board.

General answers to the questions I have posed will give the coach a starting point with respect to schedule design. The training programme must contain the following elements:

Specificity Any training programme must be highly specific to the discipline being practised. Different styles have widely differing requirements, not only in terms of technique but also in terms of the blend of 'S' factors needed to facilitate optimum performance. The schedule must take into account the individual's own capacity for work, level of commitment and involvement in the activity.

Overload Training will have a marked effect if it is systematic and progressive in ensuring that the relevant body system is overloaded. As the body system improves, so workload is commensurately increased.

Training effect Required adaptation to training comes not during the activity itself but during the period afterwards, when the body is recovering. Energy stores are replenished and muscle and other tissue are repaired or replaced. Sufficient rest must therefore be allowed between training units for this to take place. The more intense the training, the longer the period of recovery required. It is this balance between work and recovery which is the key to successful training, as opposed to straining! This is a rather important aspect and I have gone into it at slightly greater depth in the following paragraphs.

Reversibility If the training load is not progressive and/or the rest periods are set wrongly, then the student will fall back to lower levels of fitness. This, too, I have dealt with in more detail a little later in this section.

Assessment The rate of progress, or lack of it, which a student makes must be monitored. Gradings are useful indicators of this! The level of skill may also be dependent upon the components of fitness, so these also need to be regularly assessed. The coach's insight into a student's performance will be greatly helped by keeping a record of his attendance and fitness profile. Tests/assessments must be made at regular intervals and should actually monitor those elements which are specific to the discipline.

Hans Selye put forward his 'General Adaptation to Stress' theory in the 1950s. He identified an optimum stress level or workload which would bring about the maximum adaptation to training. If the load was too great, or too little, then adaptation was adversely affected. He discovered that overtraining occurred when insufficient time was allowed for recovery. Two other sports scientists named Matveev and Viru considered the cyclical approach to the training/recovery balance and put forward a theory of the periodisation of training. They observed that the recovery phase did more than restore depleted energy levels, it over-filled them. If the next work period began at the right time, this gain could be capitalised upon.

It takes time for the effects of training to appear and this means making what amount to long-term plans, centred on such things as gradings or competitions. 12-week grading intervals are actually a little on the short side for planning a thorough preparation; far better are the six-month, or one-year intervals which occur between the higher levels of advancement. However, regardless of its actual duration, we can divide our preparation time up into four allocations. These are:

1 general conditioning,

2 establishing basic technical models,

3 special conditioning,

4 establishing advanced technical models.

Though training may involve other aspects, these at least must be adequately covered.

Another way of looking at it is to see how each of the above factors build together into full preparedness on the day:

Preparation The student gradually becomes better conditioned to work at the levels required.

Adaptation The student's skills improve as a result of the training load.

Application The skills and relevant 'S' factors are finely tuned to meet the challenge.

Recuperation The body recovers from heavy training by giving an 'active' rest in which the activity or the training emphasis changes.

I have devised a very general programme which embodies these various elements. It is intended to give the coach and student a basic idea of how a 12-week period leading up to a grading might be divided up. You will note how the initial emphasis on general training changes to become more specific as the time of test draws closer.

The programme first builds the 'S' factors to the required level in the following order of emphasis:

1. Strength	2. Stamina	3. Suppleness
4. Speed	5. Skill	6. (P)Sychology

Each factor provides a base for the next, but if the student should suddenly stop all training, then the principle of reversibility comes into operation and fitness is lost in the reverse order. That is:

(P)Sychology – competition/grading preparedness
Skill – fine skill
Speed – precise timing
Suppleness – full range of movement
Stamina – the anaerobic element first
Strength – that which is specific for performance.

Planning Training

Any systematic and progressive programme of training must take into account the principles previously discussed. However, no matter how training is manipulated to bring about the desired result the essential feature is the cycle of training and overcompensation. The critical feature of this situation is the period of recovery; the muscles and other body organs must be allowed to fully get over the effects of the last training session. General speaking, training every other day, i.e. three or four times a week with a day's rest between, is ideal. This will allow the body to fully recover for the next session. But the fitter the martial artist, the faster the recovery, such that an elite performer might be able to train every day and still be fully recovered. It is for the coach to identify that the student is fully recovered prior to training.

It can be seen from diagram 5 that the ideal time to train again is during the period of overcompensation, when all the body systems and tissues have been 'over'-repaired and regenerated. The ability to train during these periods is the key to both maximum progress and performance. For the elite performer who needs to train most days and yet allow for full recovery for the next training session, the coach can manipulate the two elements of 'intensity' and 'volume' of work. Diagram 6 shows how during a week the careful coach can vary the quantity and quality of training to ensure that at the end

Diagram 4 Cycle of Overcompensation

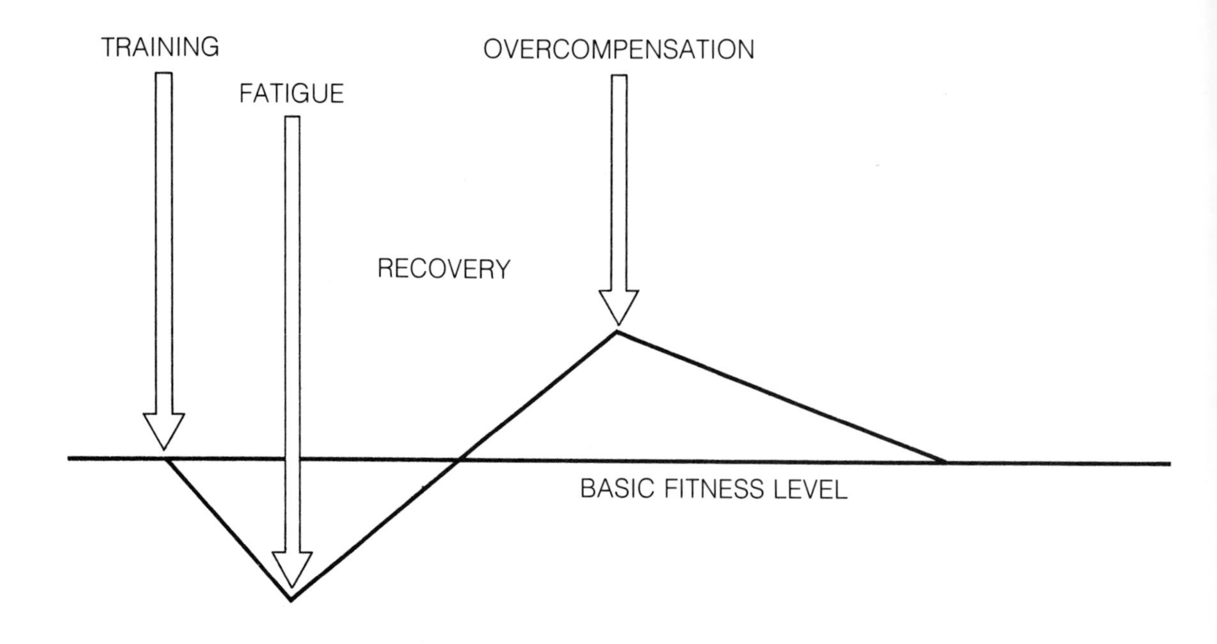

Diagram 5 Recovery and Training

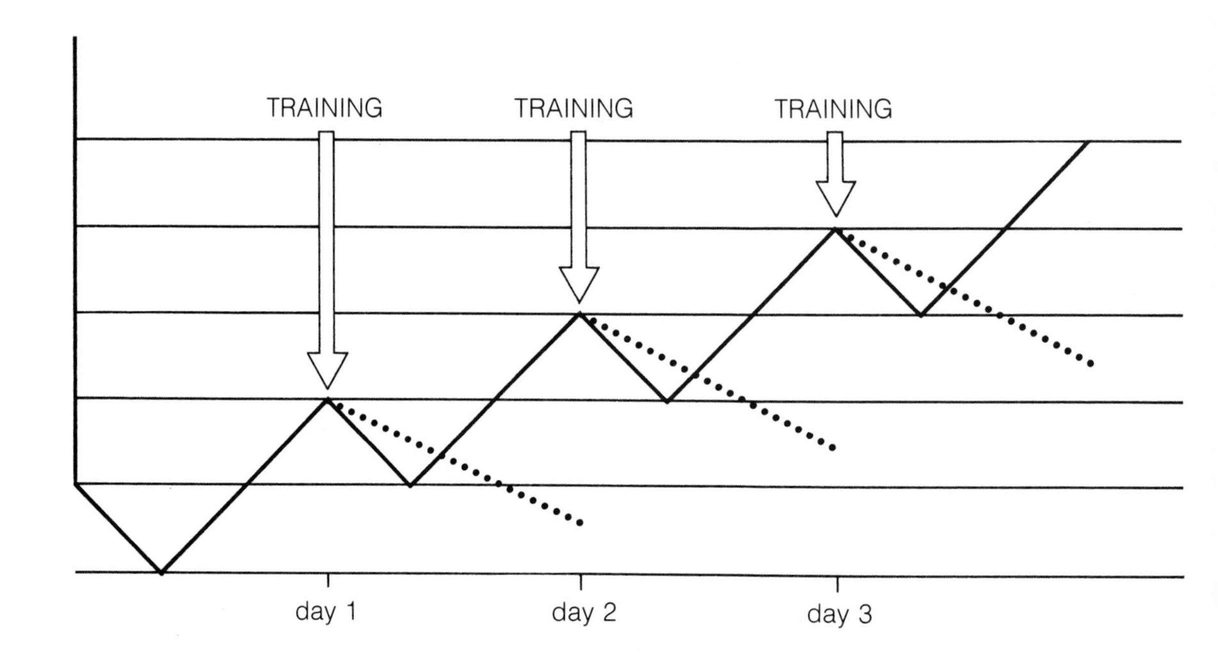

Diagram 6 The Weekly Training Programme

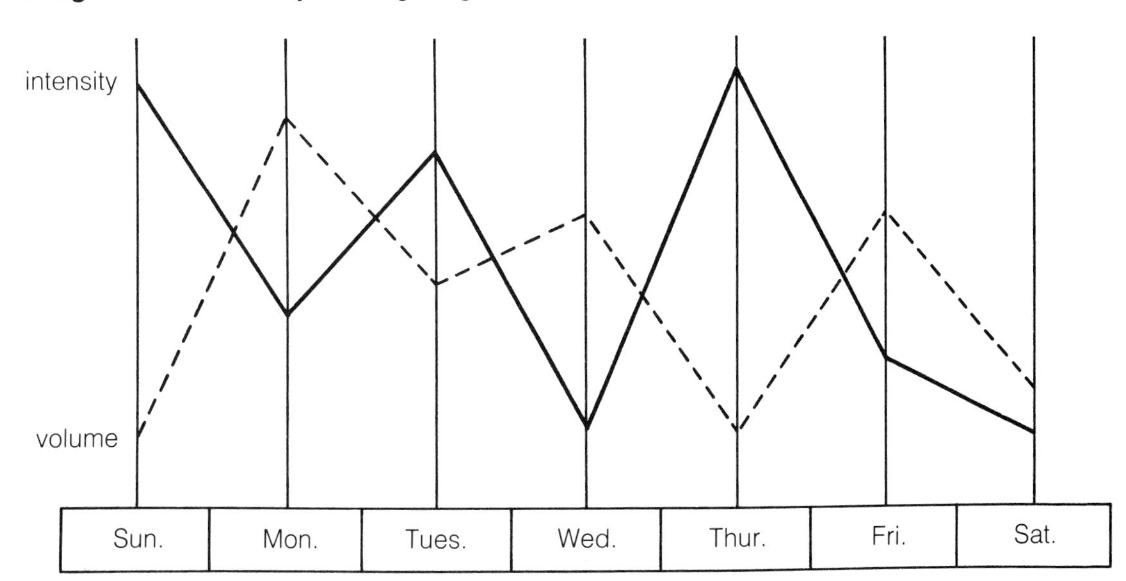

of the week the maximum benefit has been obtained from the various elements.

Each week's programme of work has also to fit into the overall plan for a twelve-week, or longer, cycle. The aim of most schedules is that on a given day in the future a student is at the peak of his ability for competition, grading or performance in general. Three phases in the programme can be identified:

1. The preparation period

Generally in this phase of training the emphasis is on general conditioning – becoming fit to train at the level required. Quantity of work as opposed to quality is the theme of lessons.

2. The pre-competition period

During this phase the emphasis changes from quantity to quality. The demands of grading, competition and performance are much more to the fore. Skills learned are honed to a fine edge, such that they can be performed in any situation. The physical demands of the stresses of these occasions are also mirrored in training.

3. The competition period

As the day or days when the high level of performance is needed draws near the emphasis in training changes to high-quality and intensity work. The very specific demands of the day/s are to the fore, such that the various pressures which the student has to cope with, as well as the high skill-level, are well rehearsed.

Diagram 7 The Twelve-week Programme (I)

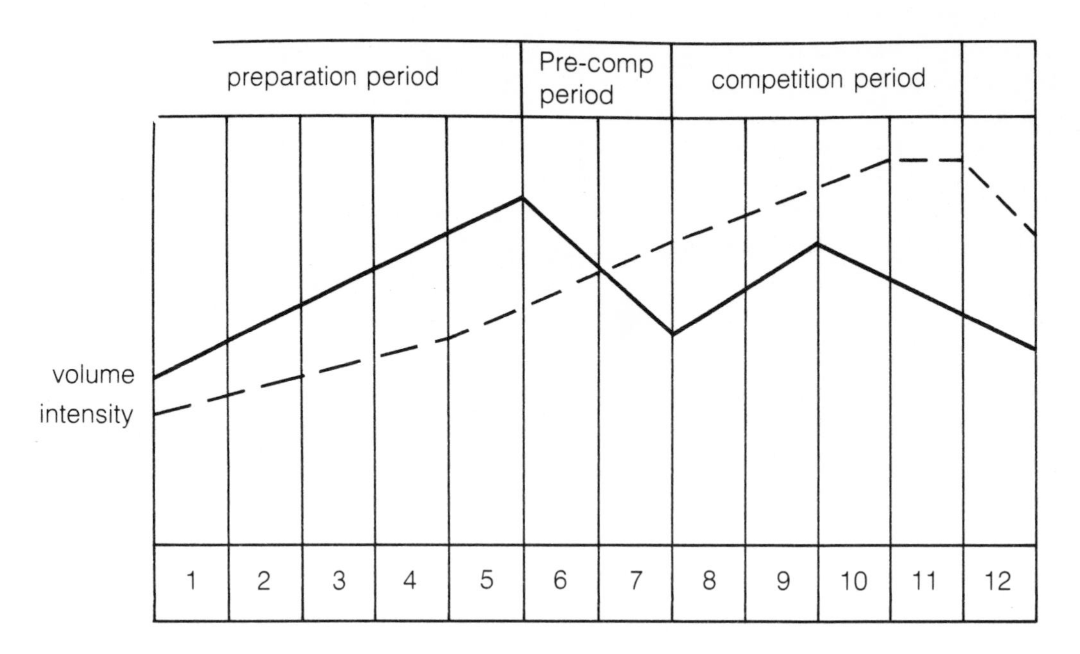

Diagram 8 The 'S' Factors and a Twelve-week Programme

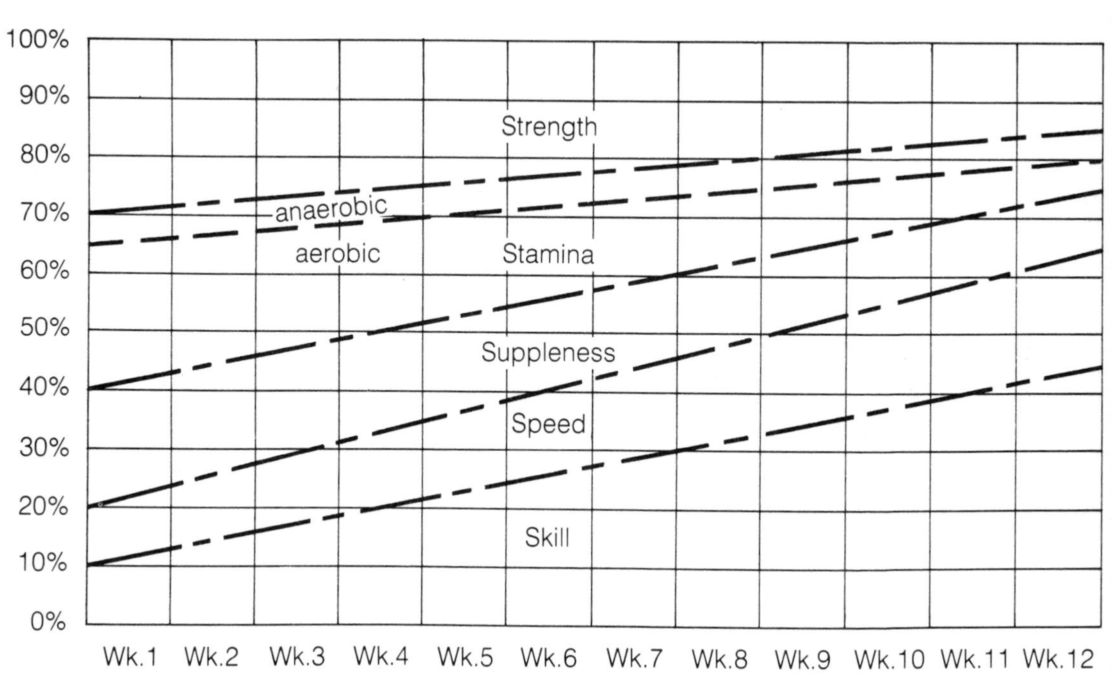

As the weeks progress, just as with the weekly programme, the volume or quantity of work and the intensity or quality of effort are manipulated to bring about the desired result. Diagram 8 shows how the various 'S' factors change in importance as the student moves from the early weeks of a programme to the final moments of preparation. Obviously no lesson is going to be split into these highly specific elements, however diagram 8 does show how the change in emphasis occurs. Diagram 9 shows how the workload changes from the very general to the highly specific. In the early stages of a programme the emphasis is on extended warm-up and basic conditioning exercises. Assuming that two or three new techniques are taught each week, as the schedule develops, more and more time is spent revising the previous week's skills and teaching new ones. Towards the latter stages of the training programme more specific elements of training might be required to develop that very fine edge of excellence.

Diagram 9 The Twelve-week Programme (II)

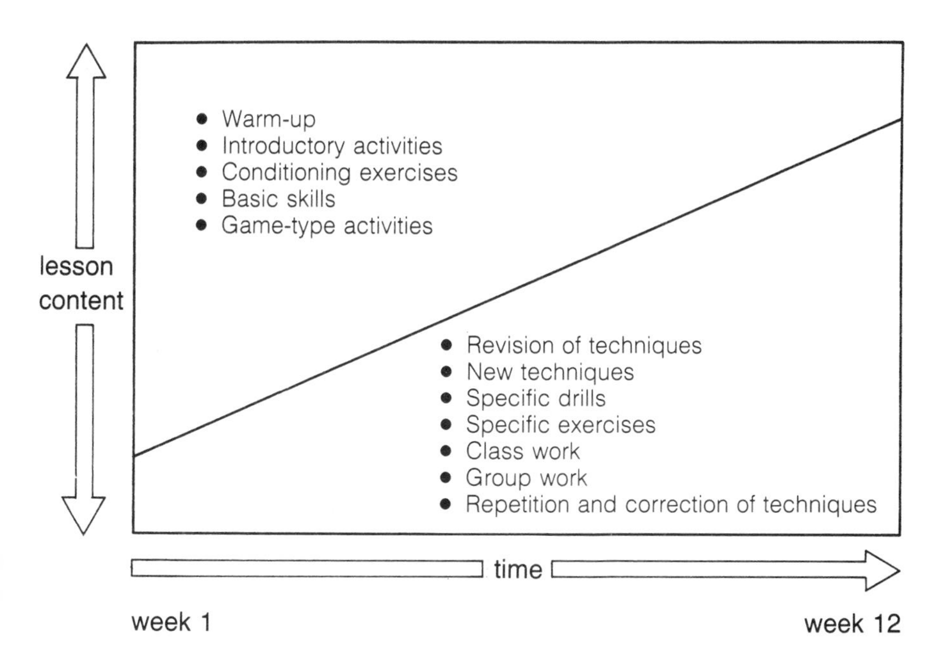

Fitness Tests and Measurements

We have already mentioned the importance of making regular and relevant assessments in order to monitor an individual's progress. We can summarise the value of such objective tests in the following manner:

- they indicate the novice's starting level of ability and skill, and provide a starting point for identifying specific areas of fitness which require attention;
- they indicate the effort which the student has made in training;
- they measure the effectiveness of a training regime, and show up any deficiencies;
- they provide the student with a source of confidence, both in his own ability and in that of the coach;
- they indicate poor form or ill-health which would be difficult to identify by other methods. It is obviously better to nip a physical or psychological problem in the bud, otherwise it may get out of hand.

I have selected some tests from among the many available. My criterion for selection has been relative reliability and simplicity of use. Only the very minimum of equipment is needed, and that is either readily available or can easily be made. The following items will be required:

- stop watch
- metre rule
- protractor
- medicine ball**
- 30-metre tape measure
- 30-centimetre rule
- pair of calipers*

* Two 30-cm rules can be bolted together
** an old football can be stuffed with rags until it weighs around 4–5 kilogrammes.

Some Tests which can be Used

Vertical Jump Test This measures the immediate and instantaneous energy pathway, as well as leg power. It obviously also measures how high a student can jump!

4 × 10-metre Shuttle Run This measures the short-term energy pathway. It also indicates how well the student can sustain speed.

10 × 10-metre Shuttle Run (from the Comprehensive Power Test) This measures the medium-term energy pathway. It also indicates speed endurance.

Three- & Five-minute Step Tests These measure medium- to long-term energy pathways. Select the one which, in terms of duration, is closer to the demands of your own discipline.

One-and-a-half mile run This measures long-term energy pathways.

Variable Step Test This measures response to different workloads.

Hamstring Flexibility Test This measures the degree of mobility in the lower back and hamstrings.

Hip Mobility Test This measures the range of movement in the pelvic girdle.

Turn-and-reach Test This measures mobility in the shoulder, lower back and pelvic girdle.

Sit-up/Press-up Tests These measure shoulder and abdominal strength and endurance.

Testing and Measuring

Any series of tests and measurements is designed to be both an indicator of the current state of fitness of an individual and of the effectiveness of a training programme. For example, if at a specific time a student is supposed to be developing mobility to help him develop specific techniques the various tests will indicate if in reality this has been achieved. If the results indicate an improvement all is well; however, if the tests indicate no improvement, or even worse a decrease in performance, then the programme will have to be reassessed or the commitment and effort of the student will have to be examined.

I would suggest that the tests might be used as follows. At the beginning of a specific period of training, over two or three training sessions, the specific 'S' factors required should be tested. This will give the coach an idea of the starting level of the student. Thereafter at regular intervals, say once a month, the tests can be repeated and the results used to assess the effectiveness of the programme and the motivation of the student. Similarly with a new student or even an experienced one a battery of tests might indicate a specific area of weakness which requires particular attention.

The tests themselves are self-explanatory with respect to the specific 'S' factors which they test. It is for the caring coach to identify those very specific elements required. The tests can be both diagnostic and add an extra element of competition to a lesson for both the group and the individuals involved. They attempt to give a score out of 100, or grade to indicate a particular level of ability at any moment in time. Obviously the aim is to improve the score next time, or to beat someone else's! Simply read off the performance against the score as with the Throwing and Jumping Decathlons, taking into account age or sex if appropriate. I would tend not to test more than three or four elements in any one session and only one if I was using the Throwing/Jumping Decathlons. I would choose, say, one power test, Vertical Jump, one mobility test, Hamstring Flexibility, one endurance test, Five-minute Step Test, and one strength test, Press-ups, in any one session per month. On subsequent retests choose the same one or similar ones for variety. By measuring four of the 'S' factors – Speed, Stamina, Suppleness and Strength – not only is the general level of fitness identified but any deficiency or superiority. But perhaps more importantly a balance or imbalance which a particular martial art requires.

The comprehensive power test in its own right is an excellent measure of all-round power, assessing leg, arms and shoulders, abdominal and general performances. Each individual element is scored as described for the individual components.

Operating the tests

1. The Vertical Jump

Stand with either the left or right side against a wall. Reach up as far as possible with the arm nearest the wall and make a mark at the highest point reached by the finger tips. Use chalk to do this. Jump as high as possible and reach up, making a second mark with the chalk. Measure the distance between the two marks.

Then, using the 'nomogram', simply mark the height achieved on the Vertical Jump column and then mark the weight of the student on the bodyweight column. Connect these two marks with a line, and read off at the point where that line crosses the power rating line. Note the reading.

Record the best of three attempts. In the example shown, a student records a best jump of 45 cms. Say the student weighs 80 kilos, you should join the point where his bodyweight is indicated in the right-hand (Bodyweight) column to the 45 cms mark in the left-hand

Fig. 167 The vertical jump. Reach as high as possible with either hand and make a mark

Fig. 168 Prepare to jump . . .

Fig. 169 . . . as high as possible making another mark

Fig. 170 Measure the distance between the two marks

(Vertical Jump) column. This is shown by the dotted line on the nomogram. Where this line crosses the central (Power Rating) column you can read off the score, in this case 60 points.

Diagram 10 The Vertical Jump Nomogram

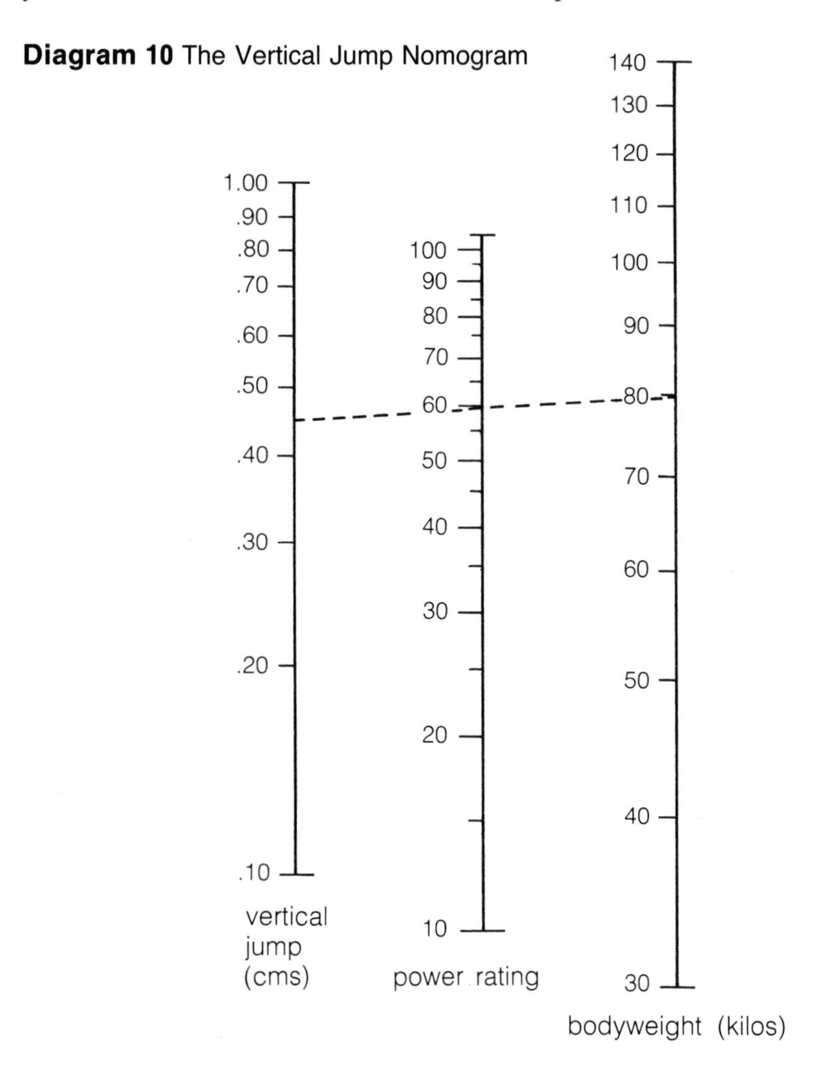

Table 5 4 × 10 metre Shuttle Run

Time (seconds)	points
8.00	100
8.05	99
8.10	98
8.15	97
8.20	96
8.25	95
8.30	94
8.35	93

Time (seconds)	points
8.40	92
8.45	91
8.50	90
8.55	89
8.60	88
8.65	87
8.70	86
8.75	85
8.80	84
8.85	83
8.90	82
8.95	81
9.00	80
9.05	79
9.10	78
9.15	77
9.20	76
9.25	75
9.30	74
9.35	73
9.40	72
9.45	71
9.50	70
9.55	69
9.60	68
9.65	67
9.70	66
9.75	65
9.80	64
9.85	63
9.90	62
9.95	61
10.00	60
10.05	59
10.10	58
10.15	57
10.20	56
10.25	55
10.30	54
10.35	53
10.40	52
10.45	51
10.50	50
10.55	49
10.60	48
10.65	47
10.70	46

Time (seconds)	points
10.75	45
10.80	44
10.85	43
10.90	42
10.95	41
11.00	40
11.05	39
11.10	38
11.15	37
11.20	36
11.25	35
11.30	34
11.35	33
11.40	32
11.45	31
11.50	30
11.55	29
11.60	28
11.65	27
11.70	26
11.75	25
11.80	24
11.85	23
11.90	22
11.95	21
12.00	20
12.05	19
12.10	18
12.15	17
12.20	16
12.25	15
12.30	14
12.35	13
12.40	12
12.45	11
12.50	10
12.55	9
12.60	8
12.65	7
12.70	6
12.75	5
12.80	4
12.85	3
12.90	2
12.95	1
13.00	0

2. The 4 × 10-metre Shuttle Run

Mark two lines 10 metres apart on the floor. The student stands with his front foot just touching the line and when ready, he sprints for the other line. He puts one foot over the far line, turns, then sprints back to the start line. Start timing as soon as his back foot breaks contact with the ground to make the first stride and stop the clock as he re-crosses the start.

If a student records a time of, say, 9.25 seconds, look down the left-hand column of the table until you find the time, and read off the score in the right-hand column, which in this case is 75 points.

Fig. 171 The standing start for the shuttle run. Front foot behind the start line

Fig. 172 During the shuttle run the foot must go over the marking line at both ends

3. The 10 × 10-metre Shuttle Run

Use the tables for the comprehensive power test (see page 157). Score as for the 4 × 10-metre shuttle run.

4(a). The Five-minute Step Test

For a time period of five minutes the student steps on and off a bench at a constant rate of thirty steps per minute. Bench height must be the same if other results are to be compared, and I recommend using a normal gymnasium bench. A metronome set at 120 counts per minute is useful for setting the pace, but experience will soon allow you to judge the rhythm accurately enough. The following sequence constitutes a complete step:

- the starting position,
- right foot on the bench,
- left follows onto bench,
- right foot steps off,
- left foot steps off.

Fig. 173 The step tests. The starting position!

Fig. 174 Right foot on bench

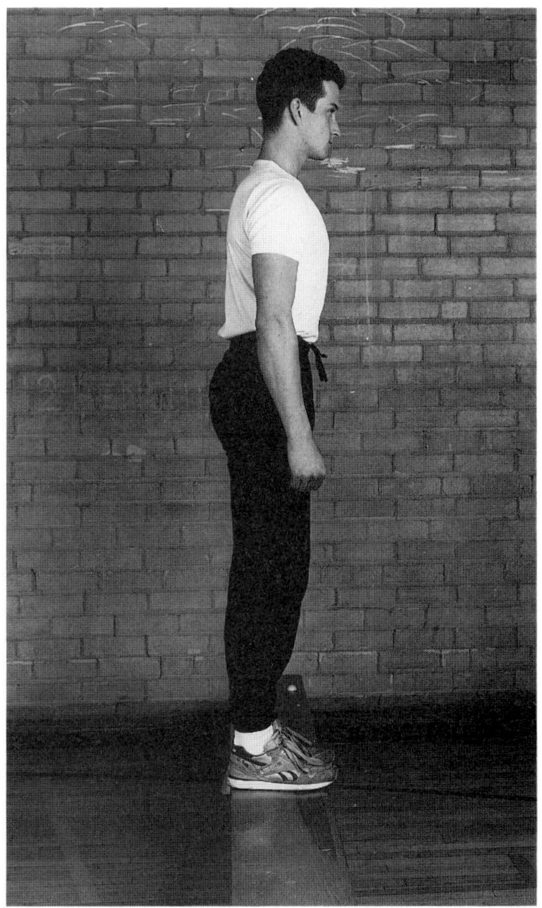

Fig. 175 Left foot on bench. Right foot off bench. Followed by the left

It is not a bad idea to change the leading foot after two and a half minutes' stepping.

When the time period expires, the student sits down and finds his pulse. One minute after stopping, the pulse is counted over a period of 60 seconds and the fitness rating read off the table below.

The important point here is to note the sex of the student, because it is important in the scoring! Having measured the pulse count in one minute find the reading in the pulse column. For example, a female student who records a minute pulse count of 123 scores 57 points. The right-hand figures represent the female pulse counts. A male with a pulse count of 93 scores 77 points.

Table 6(a) The Five-minute Step Test

Points score	male/female pulse	Points score	male/female pulse
100	70/80	99	71/
98	72/82	97	73/83
96	74/84	95	75/85
94	76/86	93	77/87
92	78/88	91	79/89
90	80/90	89	81/91
88	82/92	87	83/93
86	84/94	85	85/95
84	86/96	83	87/97
82	88/98	81	89/99
80	90/100	79	91/101
78	92/102	77	93/103
76	94/104	75	95/105
74	96/106	73	97/107
72	98/108	71	99/109
70	100/110	69	101/111
68	102/112	67	103/113
66	104/114	65	105/115
64	106/116	63	107/117
62	108/118	61	109/119
60	110/120	59	111/121
58	112/122	57	113/123
56	114/124	55	115/125
54	116/126	53	117/127
52	118/128	51	119/129
50	120/130	49	121/131
48	122/132	47	123/133
46	124/134	45	125/135
44	126/136	43	127/137
42	128/138	41	129/139
40	130/140	39	131/141
38	132/142	37	133/143
36	134/144	35	135/145
34	136/146	33	137/147
32	138/148	31	139/149
30	140/150	29	141/151
28	142/152	27	143/153
26	144/154	25	145/155
24	146/156	23	147/157
22	148/158	21	149/159
20	150/160	19	151/161
18	152/162	17	153/163

Points score	male/female pulse	Points score	male/female pulse
16	154/164	15	155/165
14	156/166	13	157/167
12	158/168	11	159/169
10	160/170	9	161/171
8	162/172	7	163/173
6	164/174	5	165/175
4	166/176	3	167/177
2	168/178	1	169/179
0	170/180		

4(b). The Three-minute Step Test

This is similar to the previous test except that its duration is reduced to three minutes and the rate changed to 25 steps per minute. A metronome set at 100 counts per minute will be helpful. Pulse is taken over a period of 60 seconds, immediately upon cessation of stepping. Read the fitness level directly from the following chart. Score in exactly the same way as the Five-minute Step Test.

Table 6b Three-minute Step Test

Points score	male/female pulse	Points score	male/female pulse
100	100/110	99	101/111
98	102/112	97	103/113
96	104/114	95	105/115
94	106/116	93	107/117
92	108/118	91	109/119
90	110/120	89	111/121
88	112/122	87	113/123
86	114/124	85	115/125
84	116/126	83	117/127
82	118/128	81	119/129
80	120/130	79	121/131
78	122/132	77	123/133
76	124/134	75	125/135
74	126/136	73	127/137
72	128/138	71	129/139
70	130/140	69	131/141
68	132/142	67	133/143
66	134/144	65	135/145

Points score	male/female pulse	Points score	male/female pulse
64	136/146	63	137/147
62	138/148	61	139/149
60	140/150	59	141/151
58	142/152	57	143/153
56	144/154	55	145/155
54	146/156	53	147/157
52	148/158	51	149/159
50	150/160	49	151/161
48	152/162	47	153/163
46	154/164	45	155/165
44	156/166	43	157/167
42	158/168	41	159/169
40	160/170	39	161/171
38	162/172	37	163/173
36	164/174	35	165/175
34	166/176	33	167/177
32	168/178	31	169/179
30	170/180	29	171/181
28	172/182	27	173/183
26	174/184	25	175/185
24	176/186	23	177/187
22	178/188	21	179/189
20	180/190	19	181/191
18	182/192	17	183/193
16	184/194	15	185/195
14	186/196	13	187/197
12	188/198	11	189/199
10	190/200	9	191/201
8	192/202	7	193/203
6	194/204	5	195/205
4	196/206	3	197/207
2	198/208	1	199/209

5. The Selective Work-intensity Step Test

This simple test is useful for assessing a student's endurance capacity at different work levels. Begin with a stepping-rate of 12 times per minute for one minute's duration. Immediately take the pulse over a 60-second interval and check the chart for an initial fitness rating. Allow the pulse to return to near-normal then repeat the exercise, this time using a stepping-rate of 18 times per minute. Check the fitness rating a second time. When the pulse is back to normal, perform the exercise again, but this time with a stepping-rate of 24 times per minute.

Table 7 Selective Work-intensity Step Test

Points score	Male/female pulse rates 12 steps/min	18 steps/min	24 steps/min
100	60/70	80/90	100/110
98	61/71	81/91	101/111
96	62/72	82/92	102/112
94	63/73	83/93	103/113
92	64/74	84/94	104/114
90	65/75	85/95	105/115
88	66/76	86/96	106/116
86	67/77	87/97	107/117
84	68/78	88/98	108/118
82	69/79	89/99	109/119
80	70/80	90/100	110/120
78	71/81	91/101	111/121
76	72/82	92/102	112/122
74	73/83	93/103	113/123
72	74/84	94/104	114/124
70	75/85	95/105	115/125
68	76/86	96/106	116/126
66	77/87	97/107	117/127
64	78/88	98/108	118/128
62	79/89	99/109	119/129
60	80/90	100/110	120/130
58	81/91	101/111	121/131
56	82/92	102/112	122/132
54	83/93	103/113	123/133
52	84/94	104/114	124/134
50	85/95	105/115	125/135
48	86/96	106/116	126/136
46	87/97	107/117	127/137
44	88/98	108/118	128/138
42	89/99	109/119	129/139
40	90/100	110/120	130/140
38	91/101	111/121	131/141
36	92/102	112/122	132/142
34	93/103	113/123	133/143
32	94/104	114/124	134/144
30	95/105	115/125	135/145
28	96/106	116/126	136/146
26	97/107	117/127	137/147
24	98/108	118/128	138/148
22	99/109	119/129	139/149
20	100/110	120/130	140/150
18	101/111	121/131	141/151
16	102/112	122/132	142/152

Points score	Male/female pulse rates 12 steps/min	18 steps/min	24 steps/min
14	103/113	123/133	143/153
12	104/114	124/134	144/154
10	105/115	125/135	145/155
8	106/116	126/136	146/156
6	107/117	127/137	147/157
4	108/118	128/138	148/158
2	109/119	129/139	149/159
1	110/120	130/140	150/160

6. The One-and-a-half Mile Run

The student must run one and a half miles on flat ground, be it on roads, grass, or 6 laps of a 400-metre track. Time the run and refer to the chart below for a fitness rating.

As with some of the previous tests the coach has to take into account the sex and age of the student. Having done that he can then obtain a score for the run. There are two separate tables for males and females – make sure you choose the right one! Each table is divided into columns to allow for the ageing process. Having found the right set of tables and the correct age column the rest should be fairly straightforward. For example, a male student who is 39 years of age records a time for 10 minutes and 11 seconds (10.11). Find the male chart and the age category 35–45, and look down that column until you find his time – 10.11. Read off his score in the left-hand column – in this case 56 points. A female aged 17 running the distance in 11.12 would score 64 points.

Table 8 One-and-a-half Mile Run

Chart for use by males

Points	Time taken (minutes/seconds) 15 to 24 yrs.	25 to 34 yrs.	35 to 44 yrs.	45 to 54 yrs.	55 to 64 yrs.	65 yrs. or over
100	08.00	08.30	09.00	09.30	10.00	10.30
99	08.01	08.31	09.01	09.31	10.01	10.31
98	08.02	08.32	09.02	09.32	10.02	10.32
97	08.03	08.33	09.03	09.33	10.03	10.33
96	08.04	08.34	09.04	09.34	10.04	10.34
95	08.05	08.35	09.05	09.35	10.05	10.35

Points	Time taken (minutes/seconds)					
	15 to 24 yrs.	25 to 34 yrs.	35 to 44 yrs.	45 to 54 yrs.	55 to 64 yrs.	65 yrs. or over
94	08.06	08.36	09.06	09.36	10.06	10.36
93	08.07	08.37	09.07	09.37	10.07	10.37
92	08.08	08.38	09.08	09.38	10.08	10.38
91	08.09	08.39	09.09	09.39	10.09	10.39
90	08.10	08.40	09.10	09.40	10.10	10.40
89	08.11.5	08.41.5	09.11.5	09.41.5	10.11.5	10.41.5
88	08.13.0	08.43.0	09.13.0	09.43.0	10.13.0	10.43.0
87	08.14.5	08.44.5	09.14.5	09.44.5	10.14.5	10.44.5
86	08.16.0	08.46.0	09.16.0	09.46.0	10.16.0	10.46.0
85	08.17.5	08.47.5	09.17.5	09.47.5	10.17.5	10.47.5
84	08.19.0	18.49.0	09.19.0	09.49.0	10.19.0	10.49.0
83	18.20.5	18.50.5	19.20.5	19.50.5	10.20.5	10.50.5
82	08.22.0	08.52.0	09.22.0	09.52.0	10.22.0	10.52.0
81	08.23.5	08.53.5	09.23.5	09.53.5	10.23.5	10.53.5
80	08.25.0	08.55.0	09.25.0	09.55.0	10.25.0	10.55.0
79	08.27	08.57	09.27	09.57	10.27	10.57
78	08.29	08.59	09.29	09.59	10.29	10.59
77	08.31	09.01	09.31	10.01	10.31	11.01
76	08.33	09.03	09.33	10.03	10.33	11.03
75	08.35	09.05	09.35	10.05	10.35	11.05
74	08.37	09.07	09.37	10.07	10.37	11.07
73	08.39	09.09	09.39	10.09	10.39	11.09
72	08.41	09.11	09.41	10.11	10.41	11.11
71	08.43	09.13	09.43	10.13	10.43	11.13
70	08.45	09.15	09.45	10.15	10.45	11.15
69	08.47	09.17	09.47	10.17	10.47	11.17
68	08.49	09.19	09.49	10.19	10.49	11.19
67	08.51	09.21	09.51	10.21	10.51	11.21
66	08.53	09.23	09.53	10.23	10.53	11.23
65	08.55	09.25	09.55	10.25	10.55	11.25
64	08.57	09.27	09.57	10.27	10.57	11.27
63	08.59	09.29	09.59	10.29	10.59	11.29
62	09.01	09.31	10.01	10.31	11.01	11.31
61	09.03	09.33	10.03	10.33	11.03	11.33
60	09.05	09.35	10.05	10.35	11.05	11.35
59	09.07	09.37	10.07	10.37	11.07	11.37
58	09.09	09.39	10.09	10.39	11.09	11.39
57	09.11	09.41	10.11	10.41	11.11	11.41
56	09.13	09.43	10.13	10.43	11.13	11.43
55	09.15	09.45	10.15	10.45	11.15	11.45
54	09.17	09.47	10.17	10.47	11.17	11.47
53	09.19	09.49	10.19	10.49	11.19	11.49
52	09.21	09.51	10.21	10.51	11.21	11.51
51	09.23	09.53	10.23	10.53	11.23	11.53
50	09.25	09.55	10.25	10.55	11.25	11.55
49	09.28	09.58	10.28	10.58	11.28	11.58
48	09.31	10.01	10.31	11.01	11.31	12.01

Points	Time taken (minutes/seconds)					
	15 to 24 yrs.	25 to 34 yrs.	35 to 44 yrs.	45 to 54 yrs.	55 to 64 yrs.	65 yrs. or over
47	09.34	10.04	10.34	11.04	11.34	12.04
46	09.37	10.07	10.37	11.07	11.37	12.07
45	09.40	10.10	10.40	11.10	11.40	12.10
44	09.43	10.13	10.43	11.13	11.43	12.13
43	09.46	10.16	10.46	11.16	11.46	12.16
42	09.49	10.19	10.49	11.19	11.49	12.19
41	09.52	10.22	10.52	11.22	11.52	12.22
40	09.55	10.25	10.55	11.25	11.55	12.25
39	10.00	10.30	11.00	11.30	12.00	12.30
38	10.05	10.35	11.05	11.35	12.05	12.35
37	10.10	10.40	11.10	11.40	12.10	12.40
36	10.15	10.45	11.15	11.45	12.15	12.45
35	10.20	10.50	11.20	11.50	12.20	12.50
34	10.25	10.55	11.25	11.55	12.25	12.55
33	10.30	11.00	11.30	12.00	12.30	13.00
32	10.35	11.05	11.35	12.05	12.35	13.05
31	10.40	11.10	11.40	12.10	12.40	13.10
30	10.45	11.15	11.45	12.15	12.45	13.15
29	10.52	11.22	11.52	12.22	12.52	13.22
28	10.59	11.29	11.59	12.29	12.59	13.29
27	11.06	11.36	12.06	12.36	13.06	13.36
26	11.13	11.43	12.13	12.43	13.13	13.43
25	11.20	11.50	12.20	12.50	13.20	13.50
24	11.27	11.57	12.27	12.57	13.27	13.57
23	11.34	12.04	12.34	13.04	13.34	14.04
22	11.41	12.11	12.41	13.11	13.41	14.11
21	11.48	12.18	12.48	13.18	13.48	14.18
20	11.55	12.25	12.55	13.25	13.55	14.25
19	12.06	12.36	13.06	13.36	14.06	14.36
18	12.17	12.47	13.17	13.47	14.17	14.47
17	12.28	12.58	13.28	13.58	14.28	14.58
16	12.39	13.09	13.39	14.09	14.39	15.09
15	12.50	13.20	13.50	14.20	14.50	15.20
14	13.01	13.31	14.01	14.31	15.01	15.31
13	13.12	13.42	14.12	14.42	15.12	15.42
12	13.23	13.53	14.23	14.53	15.23	15.53
11	13.34	14.04	14.34	15.04	15.34	16.04
10	13.45	14.15	14.45	15.15	15.45	16.15
9	14.00	14.30	15.00	15.30	16.00	16.30
8	14.15	14.45	15.15	15.45	16.15	16.45
7	14.30	15.00	15.30	16.00	16.30	17.00
6	14.45	15.15	15.45	16.15	16.45	17.15
5	15.00	15.30	16.00	16.30	17.00	17.30
4	15.15	15.45	16.15	16.45	17.15	17.45
3	15.30	16.00	16.30	17.00	17.30	18.00
2	15.45	16.15	16.45	17.15	17.45	18.15
1	16.00	16.30	17.00	17.30	18.00	18.30
0	16.15	16.45	17.15	17.45	18.15	18.45

Chart for use by females

Points	Time taken (minutes/seconds)					
	15 to 24 yrs.	25 to 34 yrs.	35 to 44 yrs.	45 to 54 yrs.	55 to 64 yrs.	65 yrs. or over
100	10.15	10.45	11.15	11.45	12.15	12.45
99	10.16	10.46	11.16	11.46	12.16	12.46
98	10.17	10.47	11.17	11.47	12.17	12.47
97	10.18	10.48	11.18	11.48	12.18	12.48
96	10.19	10.49	11.19	11.49	12.19	12.49
95	10.20	10.50	11.20	11.50	12.20	12.50
94	10.21	10.51	11.21	11.51	12.21	12.51
93	10.22	10.52	11.22	11.52	12.22	12.52
92	10.23	10.53	11.23	11.53	12.23	12.53
91	10.24	10.54	11.24	11.54	12.24	12.54
90	10.25	10.55	11.25	11.55	12.25	12.55
89	10.26.5	10.56.5	11.26.5	11.56.5	12.26.5	12.56.5
88	10.28.0	10.58.0	11.28.0	11.58.0	12.28.0	12.58.0
87	10.29.5	10.59.5	11.29.5	11.59.5	12.29.5	12.59.5
86	10.31.0	11.01.0	11.31.0	12.01.0	12.31.0	13.01.0
85	10.32.5	11.02.5	11.32.5	12.02.5	12.32.5	13.02.5
84	10.34.0	11.04.0	11.34.0	12.04.0	12.34.0	13.04.0
83	10.35.5	11.05.5	11.35.5	12.05.5	12.35.5	13.05.5
82	10.37.0	11.07.0	11.37.0	12.07.0	12.37.0	13.07.0
81	10.38.5	11.08.5	11.38.5	12.08.5	12.38.5	13.08.5
80	10.40.0	11.10.0	11.40.0	12.10.0	12.40.0	13.10.0
79	10.42	11.12	11.42	12.12	12.42	13.12
78	10.44	11.14	11.44	12.14	12.44	13.14
77	10.46	11.16	11.46	12.16	12.46	13.16
76	10.48	11.18	11.48	12.18	12.48	13.18
75	10.50	11.20	11.50	12.20	12.50	13.20
74	10.52	11.22	11.52	12.22	12.52	13.22
73	10.54	11.24	11.54	12.24	12.54	13.24
72	10.56	11.26	11.56	12.26	12.56	13.26
71	10.58	11.28	11.58	12.28	12.58	13.28
70	11.00	11.30	12.00	12.30	13.00	13.30
69	11.02	11.32	12.02	12.32	13.02	13.32
68	11.04	11.34	12.04	12.34	13.04	13.34
67	11.06	11.36	12.06	12.36	13.06	13.36
66	11.08	11.38	12.08	12.38	13.08	13.38
65	11.10	11.40	12.10	12.40	13.10	13.40
64	11.12	11.42	12.12	12.42	13.12	13.42
63	11.14	11.44	12.14	12.44	13.14	13.44
62	11.16	11.46	12.16	12.46	13.16	13.46
61	11.18	11.48	12.18	12.48	13.18	13.48
60	11.20	11.50	12.20	12.50	13.20	13.50
59	11.22	11.52	12.22	12.52	13.22	13.52
58	11.24	11.54	12.24	12.54	13.24	13.54
57	11.26	11.56	12.26	12.56	13.26	13.56
56	11.28	11.58	12.28	12.58	13.28	13.58
55	11.30	12.00	12.30	13.00	13.30	14.00

Points	Time taken (minutes/seconds)					
	15 to 24 yrs.	25 to 34 yrs.	35 to 44 yrs.	45 to 54 yrs.	55 to 64 yrs.	65 yrs. or over
54	11.32	12.02	12.32	13.02	13.32	14.02
53	11.34	12.04	12.34	13.04	13.34	14.04
52	11.36	12.06	12.36	13.06	13.36	14.06
51	11.38	12.08	12.38	13.08	13.38	14.08
50	11.40	12.10	12.40	13.10	13.40	14.10
49	11.42	12.12	12.42	13.12	13.42	14.12
48	11.45	12.15	12.45	13.15	13.45	14.15
47	11.48	12.18	12.48	13.18	13.48	14.18
46	11.51	12.21	12.51	13.21	13.51	14.21
45	11.54	12.24	12.54	13.24	13.54	14.24
44	11.57	12.27	12.57	13.27	13.57	14.27
43	12.00	12.30	13.00	13.30	14.00	14.30
42	12.03	12.33	13.03	13.33	14.03	14.33
41	12.06	12.36	13.06	13.36	14.06	14.36
40	12.11	12.41	13.11	13.41	14.11	14.41
39	12.16	12.46	13.16	14.46	14.16	14.46
38	12.21	12.51	13.21	13.51	14.21	14.51
37	12.26	12.56	13.26	13.56	14.26	14.56
36	12.31	13.01	13.31	14.01	14.31	15.01
35	12.36	13.06	13.36	14.06	14.36	15.06
34	12.41	13.11	13.41	14.11	14.41	15.11
33	12.46	13.16	13.46	14.16	14.46	15.16
32	12.51	13.21	13.51	14.21	14.51	15.21
31	12.56	13.26	13.56	14.26	14.56	15.26
30	13.03	13.33	14.03	14.33	15.03	15.33
29	13.10	13.40	14.10	14.40	15.10	15.40
28	13.17	13.47	14.17	14.47	15.17	15.47
27	13.24	13.54	14.24	14.54	15.24	15.54
26	13.31	14.01	14.31	15.01	15.31	16.01
25	13.38	14.08	14.38	15.08	15.38	16.08
24	13.45	14.15	14.45	15.15	15.45	16.15
23	13.52	14.22	14.52	15.22	15.52	16.22
22	13.59	14.29	14.59	15.29	15.59	16.29
21	14.06	14.36	15.06	15.36	16.06	16.36
20	14.17	14.47	15.17	15.47	16.17	16.47
19	14.28	14.58	15.28	15.58	16.28	16.58
18	14.39	15.09	15.39	16.09	16.39	17.09
17	14.50	15.20	15.50	16.20	16.50	17.20
16	15.01	15.31	16.01	16.31	17.01	17.31
15	15.12	15.42	16.12	16.42	17.12	17.42
14	15.23	15.53	16.23	16.53	17.23	17.53
13	15.34	16.04	16.34	17.04	17.34	18.04
12	15.45	16.15	16.45	17.15	17.45	18.15
11	16.00	16.30	17.00	17.30	18.00	18.30
10	16.15	16.45	17.15	17.45	18.15	18.45
9	16.30	17.00	17.30	18.00	18.30	19.00
8	16.45	17.15	17.45	18.15	18.45	19.15

Points	Time taken (minutes/seconds)					
	15 to 24 yrs.	25 to 34 yrs.	35 to 44 yrs.	45 to 54 yrs.	55 to 64 yrs.	65 yrs. or over
7	17.00	17.30	18.00	18.30	19.00	19.30
6	17.15	17.45	18.15	18.45	19.15	19.45
5	17.30	18.00	18.30	19.00	19.30	20.00
4	17.45	18.15	18.45	19.15	19.45	20.15
3	18.00	18.30	19.00	19.30	20.00	20.30
2	18.15	18.45	19.15	19.45	20.15	20.45
1	18.30	19.00	19.30	20.00	20.30	21.00
0	18.45	19.15	19.45	20.15	20.45	21.15

7. Lower-back and Hamstring Flexibility

Stand on a bench or step with your legs straight. Reach forward to touch your toes. Measure the distance above or below the bench that you can reach. A plus sign in front of the measurement means that

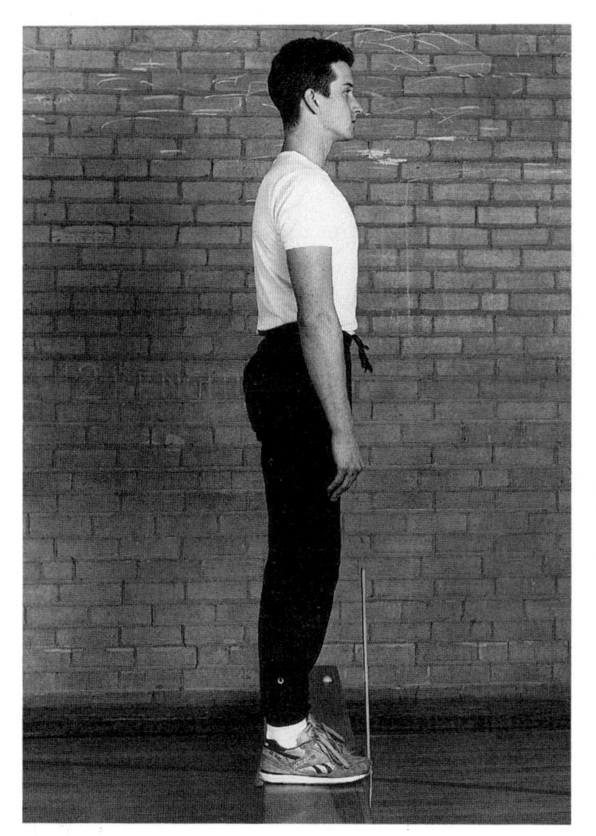

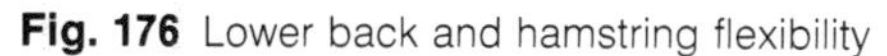

Fig. 176 Lower back and hamstring flexibility

Fig. 177 Keep the legs straight

Fig. 178 Reach as far down the scale as possible

your fingertips have extended below the bench. A minus sign means that you have reached to a point above the bench. Find your best distance (of three attempts) on the left-hand column, (Reach distance), and read off your score on the right.

Table 9 Lower-back and Hamstring Flexibility

Reach distance	Points	Reach distance	Points
+25.0	100	+24.5	99
+24.0	98	+23.5	97
+23.0	96	+22.5	95
+22.0	94	+21.5	93
+21.0	92	+20.5	91
+20.0	90	+19.5	89
+19.0	88	+18.5	87
+18.0	86	+17.5	85
+17.0	84	+16.5	83
+16.0	82	+15.5	81
+15.0	80	+14.5	79
+14.0	78	+13.5	77
+13.0	76	+12.5	75
+12.0	74	+11.5	73

Reach distance	Points	Reach distance	Points
+11.0	72	+10.5	71
+10.0	70	+ 9.5	69
+ 9.0	68	+ 8.5	67
+ 8.0	66	+ 7.5	65
+ 7.0	64	+ 6.5	63
+ 6.0	62	+ 5.5	61
+ 5.0	60	+ 4.5	59
+ 4.0	58	+ 3.5	57
+ 3.0	56	+ 2.5	55
+ 2.0	54	+ 1.5	53
+ 1.0	52	+ 0.5	51
0.0	50	− 0.5	49
− 1.0	48	− 1.5	47
− 2.0	46	− 2.5	45
− 3.0	44	− 3.5	43
− 4.0	42	− 4.5	41
− 5.0	40	− 5.5	39
− 6.0	38	− 6.5	37
− 7.0	36	− 7.5	35
− 8.0	34	− 8.5	33
− 9.0	32	− 9.5	31
−10.0	30	−10.5	29
−11.0	28	−11.5	27
−12.0	26	−12.5	25
−13.0	24	−13.5	23
−14.0	22	−14.5	21
−15.0	20	−15.5	19
−16.0	18	−16.5	17
−17.0	16	−17.5	15
−18.0	14	−18.5	13
−19.0	12	−19.5	11
−20.0	10	−20.5	9
−21.0	8	−21.5	7
−22.0	6	−22.5	5
−23.0	4	−23.5	3
−24.0	2	−24.5	1
−25.0	0		

8. Hip Mobility

Sit on the floor and open your legs as wide as possible. Place the calipers tight into the crotch, so they run along the inside of the thighs. Adjust them to the correct angle, then remove and read off the angle with a protractor. Score as with lower-back and hamstring test.

Fig. 179 Split the legs as wide as possible. Lay the dividers along the inside of the legs

Fig. 180 Read off the angle

Table 10 Hip Mobility

Score	Degrees	Score	Degrees
100	180	99	178.5
98	177	97	175.5
96	174	95	172.5
94	171	93	169.5
92	168	91	166.5
90	165	89	163.5

Score	Degrees	Score	Degrees
88	162	87	160.5
86	159	85	157.5
84	156	83	154.5
82	153	81	151.5
80	150	79	148.5
78	147	77	145.5
76	144	75	142.5
74	141	73	139.5
72	138	71	136.5
70	135	69	133.5
68	132	67	130.5
66	129	65	127.5
64	126	63	124.5
62	123	61	121.5
60	120	59	118.5
58	117	57	115.5
56	114	55	112.5
54	111	53	109.5
52	108	51	106.5
50	105	49	103.5
48	102	47	100.5
46	99	45	97.5
44	96	43	94.5
42	93	41	91.5
40	90	39	88.5
38	87	37	85.5
36	84	35	82.5
34	81	33	79.5
32	78	31	76.5
30	75	29	73.5
28	72	27	70.5
26	69	25	67.5
24	66	23	64.5
22	63	21	61.5
20	60	19	58.5
18	57	17	55.5
16	54	15	52.5
14	51	13	49.5
12	48	11	46.5
10	45	9	43.5
8	42	7	40.5
6	39	5	37.5
4	36	3	34.5
2	33	1	31.5
0	30		

9. Shoulder, Trunk and Hip Flexibility

Draw a line on the floor at right angles to, and extended vertically up, a wall. Stand with both feet just touching the line, with the left side nearest the wall. Stretch out the right arm and twist around, so the hand touches the wall. Measure the distance reached before or beyond the line. Before the line measurements are prefixed, with a minus sign, and beyond the line with a plus sign. The feet do not turn with the shoulders and trunk. Score as with the other mobility tests.

Measure left side mobility by standing with your right side nearest the wall.

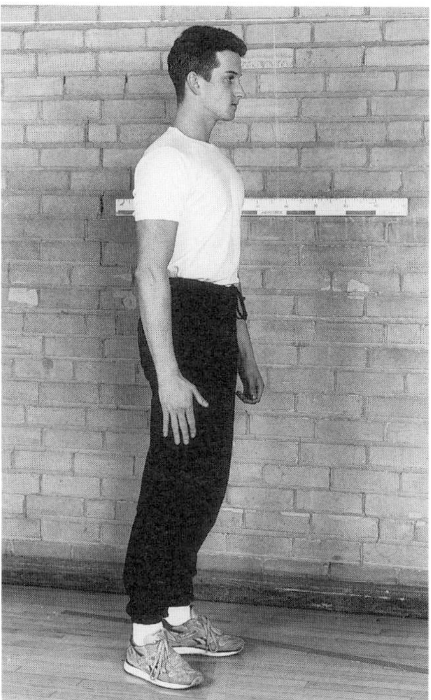

Fig. 181 Turning to the right. The feet placement can be reversed to measure the turn to the left

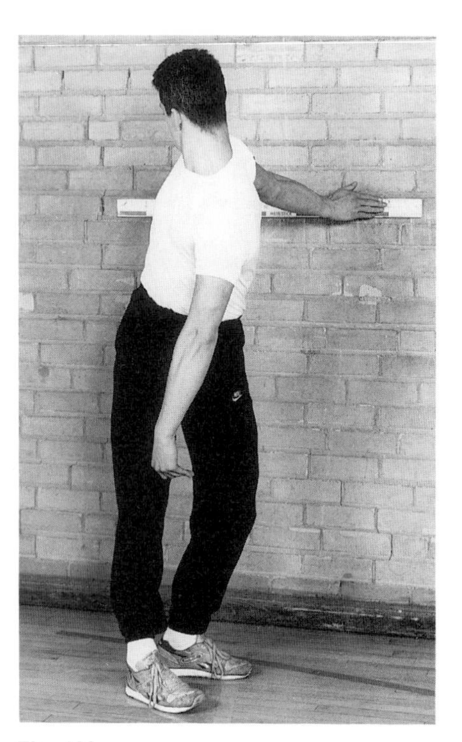

Fig. 182

Table 11 Shoulder, Trunk and Hip Flexibility

Score	Distance	Score	Distance
100	+1.00	99	+0.98
98	+0.96	97	+0.94
96	+0.92	95	+0.90
94	+0.88	93	+0.86
92	+0.84	91	+0.82
90	+0.80	89	+0.78

Score	Distance	Score	Distance
88	+0.76	87	+0.74
86	+0.72	85	+0.70
84	+0.68	83	+0.66
82	+0.64	81	+0.62
80	+0.60	79	+0.58
78	+0.56	77	+0.54
76	+0.52	75	+0.50
74	+0.48	73	+0.46
72	+0.44	71	+0.42
70	+0.40	69	+0.38
68	+0.36	67	+0.34
66	+0.32	65	+0.30
64	+0.28	63	+0.26
62	+0.24	61	+0.22
60	+0.20	59	+0.18
58	+0.16	57	+0.14
56	+0.12	55	+0.10
54	+0.08	53	+0.06
52	+0.04	51	+0.02
50	0.00	49	+0.02
48	−0.04	47	−0.06
46	−0.08	45	−0.10
44	−0.12	43	−0.14
42	−0.16	41	−0.18
40	−0.20	39	−0.22
38	−0.24	37	−0.26
36	−0.28	35	−0.30
34	−0.32	33	−0.34
32	−0.36	31	−0.38
30	−0.40	29	−0.42
28	−0.44	27	−0.46
26	−0.48	25	−0.50
24	−0.52	23	−0.54
22	−0.56	21	−0.58
20	−0.60	19	−0.62
18	−0.64	17	−0.66
16	−0.68	15	−0.70
14	−0.72	13	−0.74
12	−0.76	11	−0.78
10	−0.80	9	−0.82
8	−0.84	7	−0.86
6	−0.88	5	−0.90
4	−0.92	3	−0.94
2	−0.96	1	−0.98
0	−1.00		

Fig. 183 The classic starting position for the press-up. The chest is lowered to the floor each time

Fig. 184 The bent leg sit-up

10. Abdominal and Shoulder Strength

Perform the standard Press-up, keeping your back and legs straight. Bend your elbows so your nose touches the floor. Count the number of complete Press-ups performed in 60 seconds. No pauses or rests are allowed. Modified Press-ups in which the knees touch the floor can be used if necessary, though this modification must be taken into account when making comparisons.

Having counted the number of Press-ups or abdominals in one minute the coach also needs to note the age and sex of the student. Again, there are two separate tables for males and females, the left-hand column of each indicating the age category. For example, a male student aged 25 achieving 40 Press-ups would find himself in the 'C' category. Always go to the category below if the score does not exactly match the tables. For example, a 35-year-old female achieving 36 abdominals would be in the 'B' category.

Perform Bent Leg Sit-ups with your hands behind your head and the feet anchored. Sit-up until your elbows touch your knees. Count the number of complete Sit-ups performed in 60 seconds and allow no rests or pauses.

Table 12(a) Abdominal Strength

Abdominals

	Age	Fitness group				
		A	B	C	D	E
Males	15–24	70+	60	50	40	30
	25–34	58+	48	38	28	18
	35–44	48+	38	28	18	13
	45–54	38+	28	23	13	8
	55–64	33+	23	18	10	3
	65 or over	28+	18	13	6	1

Number of abdominals

	Age	Fitness group				
		A	B	C	D	E
Females	15–24	58+	48	38	28	20
	25–34	48+	38	28	18	8
	35–44	43+	33	23	13	6
	45–54	33+	23	18	10	4
	55–64	28+	21	12	5	2
	65 or over	23+	16	10	3	1

Number of abdominals

Table 12(b) Shoulder Strength

Shoulder Strength

	Age	Fitness group A	B	C	D	E
Males	15–24	70+	60	50	40	30
	25–34	60+	50	40	30	20
	35–44	50+	40	30	20	15
	45–54	40+	30	25	15	10
	55–64	35+	25	20	12	5
	65 or over	30+	20	15	8	3

Number of press-ups

	Age	Fitness group A	B	C	D	E
Females	15–24	60+	50	40	30	20
	25–34	50+	40	30	20	10
	35–44	45+	35	25	15	8
	45–54	35+	25	20	12	6
	55–64	30+	23	14	7	4
	65 or over	25+	18	12	6	2

Number of press-ups

11. The Comprehensive Power Test

This test is composed of four elements, each one designed to measure the performance of a particular part of the body. For this purpose the tests are as follows:

Vertical Jump – legs
Press-ups – arms and shoulders
Sit-ups – abdominals and trunk
10 × 10-metre Shuttle Run – general body agility

These tests are drawn from others in this section and are designed to assess all-round power. Easily organised in less than five minutes, an individual's ability can be assessed in a comprehensive fashion including legs, arms, abdominals and all-round agility.

The Vertical Jump

As before, record the best of three attempts, find the appropriate column, follow it down until you find the distance jumped and read off the score in the left-hand column. For example, a jump of 66cms, gives a score of 66 points.

Press-ups
The maximum number of standard Press-ups in a minute is recorded. Again, look down the appropriate column until you find the number achieved and read off the score on the far left-hand side. For example, 47 Press-ups give a score of 67 points.

The Shuttle Run
A timed run over 10 × 10 metres (100m in total) is performed. It should be started, timed and organised in the same way as the 4 × 10. For example, a time of 24.60 would give a score of 59 points.

Sit-ups
The maximum number of Sit-ups in one minute is noted. The procedure for scoring is similar to that of Press-ups. So, for example, 51 Abdominals would give a score of 71 points.

For a well-conditioned student there should be some measure of equality between the four scores, to indicate a well-balanced state of fitness.

Table 13 Comprehensive Power Test

Score	Vertical Jump (cms)	Press-ups (per 60 secs.)	10 × 10m. Shuttle (secs.)	Sit-ups (per 60 secs.)
100	1.00	80	20.00	80
99	0.99	79	20.10	79
98	0.98	78	20.20	78
97	0.97	77	20.30	77
96	0.96	76	20.40	76
95	0.95	75	20.50	75
94	0.94	74	20.60	74
93	0.93	73	20.70	73
92	0.92	72	20.80	72
91	0.91	71	20.90	71
90	0.90	70	21.00	70
89	0.89	69	21.10	69
88	0.88	68	21.20	68
87	0.87	67	21.30	67
86	0.86	66	21.40	66
85	0.85	65	21.50	65
84	0.84	64	21.60	64
83	0.83	63	21.70	63

Score	Vertical Jump (cms)	Press-ups (per 60 secs.)	10 × 10m. Shuttle (secs.)	Sit-ups (per 60 secs.)
82	0.82	62	21.80	62
81	0.81	61	21.90	61
80	0.80	60	22.00	60
79	0.79	59	22.10	59
78	0.78	58	22.20	58
77	0.77	57	22.30	57
76	0.76	56	22.40	56
75	0.75	55	22.50	55
74	0.74	54	22.60	54
73	0.73	53	22.70	53
72	0.72	52	22.80	52
71	0.71	51	22.90	51
70	0.70	50	23.00	50
69	0.69	49	23.15	49
68	0.68	48	23.30	48
67	0.67	47	23.45	47
66	0.66	46	23.60	46
65	0.65	45	23.75	45
64	0.64	44	23.90	44
63	0.63	43	24.00	43
62	0.62	42	24.15	42
61	0.61	41	24.30	41
60	0.60	40	24.45	40
59	0.59	39	24.60	39
58	0.58	38	24.75	38
57	0.57	37	24.90	37
56	0.56	36	25.00	36
55	0.55	35	25.15	35
54	0.54	34	25.30	34
53	0.53	33	25.45	33
52	0.52	32	25.60	32
51	0.51	31	25.75	31
50	0.50	30	25.90	30
49	0.49	29	26.00	29
48	0.48	28	26.15	28
47	0.47	27	26.30	27
46	0.46	26	26.45	26
45	0.45	25	26.60	25
44	0.44	24	26.75	24
43	0.43	23	26.90	23
42	0.42	22	27.00	22
41	0.41	21	27.15	21
40	0.40	20	27.30	20
39	0.39	**	27.45	**
38	0.38	19	27.60	19
37	0.37	**	27.75	**
36	0.36	18	27.90	18
35	0.35	**	28.00	**

Score	Vertical Jump (cms)	Press-ups (per 60 secs.)	10 × 10m. Shuttle (secs.)	Sit-ups (per 60 secs.)
34	0.34	17	28.15	17
33	0.33	**	28.30	**
32	0.32	16	28.45	16
31	0.31	**	28.60	**
30	0.30	15	28.75	15
29	0.29	**	29.00	**
28	0.28	14	29.15	14
27	0.27	**	29.30	**
26	0.26	13	29.45	13
25	0.25	**	29.60	**
24	0.24	12	29.75	12
23	0.23	**	29.90	**
22	0.22	11	30.00	11
21	0.21	**	30.15	**
20	0.20	10	30.30	10
19	0.19	**	30.45	**
18	0.18	9	30.60	9
17	0.17	**	30.75	**
16	0.16	8	31.00	8
15	0.15	**	31.15	**
14	0.14	7	31.30	7
13	0.13	**	31.45	**
12	0.12	6	31.60	6
11	0.11	**	31.75	**
10	0.10	5	31.90	5
9	0.09	**	32.00	**
8	0.08	4	32.15	4
7	0.07	**	32.30	**
6	0.06	3	32.45	3
5	0.05	**	32.60	**
4	0.04	2	32.75	2
3	0.03	**	32.90	**
2	0.02	1	33.00	1
1	0.01	**	33.15	**

*Asterisks mean that there is no score for half a press-up or for half a centimetre in the vertical jump. Students should score on the nearest complete press-up and/or centimetre.